Acclaim

M000189611

MISSING INSECTS

MISSING INSECTS

Naomi M Rosenthal

NaoMinRose
Berkeley MMXI

other books by Naomi M Rosenthal

Searching for Hugo

Lina's Love: Postcards & Poems from Hugo

Dedicated to my loving grandmother, Lina
and to all people who are treated unjustly

Some people's names have been changed to protect their
privacy. Everything else is true to my memories and journals. I
chose to share many of my experiences; others I kept private.

Table of Contents

STRANGE TIMES

CREATING JOY

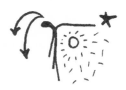

Preface

How can you know what isn't there if you've never experienced it? It would be like trying to comprehend a third dimension when you're living in a two-dimensional world.

Thus I wasn't aware of the absence of insects in my environment until I experienced their abundance in Africa. I also didn't know what was amiss during my childhood in Israel, Germany, and various parts of the US, but I felt something wasn't right in my family and knew I had to get away. Determined to experience life fully, I hitchhiked through a dozen sub-Saharan African countries and lived in different parts of the world. It was only decades later, after uncovering hidden clues in my family and putting the pieces together, that I realized how historical traumas had warped my parents' realities. At last I understood the burden that my brother and I had inherited. Now my struggles to free myself and choose a healthier existence finally made sense.

I started out writing a collection of glimpses, then saw the patterns running throughout and realized that the whole story had to be told. The result is this sometimes tragic, sometimes hilarious book.

Acknowledgements

I would like to thank the following kind people for their invaluable support in the creation of this book:

My wonderful writing teacher and editor, Linda Glaser.

Hope Richardson for proofreading the earlier version.

Susan Heileman, Joanna Katz, Emily Loeb, Steve Rosenstein, Jack Rosenthal, and Ernie Scheuer for reading the initial manuscript, offering helpful comments and suggestions, and putting up with my kvetching.

And last but not least, my friend Rose Green, for still writing at age 95 and inspiring me to keep at it.

Of course, any and all mistakes are mine.

Beginnings

First

It was a long time ago, when we lived in that little house in Ramat Gan. The memories are not continuous. They are little glimpses of light between darkness, like the way the world looked through the bars of my crib . . . pieces of light between slots of dark. I was looking at a gecko on the wall. I never saw him move, but when I forgot to look, or maybe just turned my head for an instant or blinked my eyes, and then looked again, he was in a different position. I tried to see the lizards move, trying to remember not to look away, not to forget or fall asleep, but I never succeeded.

The house was tiny. There was a bathroom, and a room in front where we ate and my brother and I slept, and my parents' room in back. That was all. It was dark much of the time. I spent long hours in my crib in the dark. I wanted something. Was it a drink of water, or had I had another bad dream? It was wrong to trouble my mother. I mustn't call her. I remember whispering very softly, "Ima, Ima." I wanted her to come, but mustn't disturb her.

I remember my mother lighting the wood fire in the bathroom for our bath. One time, while she was busy doing this, I tried to pee standing up, like my brother Hanan did. I was surprised that instead of landing in the toilet, my pee wet Hanan's sock, which was lying on the floor. Another time, as my mother was lifting me up from a stool on which I was perched, I accidentally kicked the stool over. It hit her foot, and she put me down and rubbed the sore spot. I was overcome with the horror of what I had done, of hurting my mother, and burst into tears.

I remember Outside. There was a wire fence between our house and the next, and there was a place where the mesh was torn. I used to play with the kids next door, and would sneak through the opening. This was very scary because of the landlord. If he ever caught you going through the hole in the fence, something terrible would happen. I never found out what, exactly or why, but it was very dangerous climbing through there. I was always scared when I did it. Still, none of us kids bothered to go the long way around.

When I turned four, we moved to another town, to a three story apartment building with electricity. Just after we moved, we went back to the old place. I don't know why. There were new people living there. The house was different. The people who lived there had such exotic things. I remember a painting on the wall in the front room. It had glowing, jewel-like colors painted on a shimmering black velvet surface. I was sure they were rich, the people who had moved into our little house and transformed it with their beautiful things.

Night Vision

The same dream came many times. I was walking in a barren, desert-like place with my Aunt Herta. We came to a lone stone house with an arched doorway. Silently, she left me there, and as I watched her walk away and disappear in the distance, a desolate feeling engulfed me. I entered the house. The front room had a wall with a hole in it, and a circus clown's face stuck out of the hole.

"This is not a place for children," he told me. "You must leave."

"Just a minute," I said. "I'll leave in just a minute."

I had no place else to go, and was just trying to postpone the inevitable horror of being cast out. Then the scene changed. It was the same house, but now I was with my parents, so it was OK to be there. A waiter seated us at a table in another room and brought us ice cream.

In another dream, a witch was intent on killing me. She was made of green paper, so I tore her up, but found I couldn't destroy the pieces, and couldn't get rid of her.

I was afraid of going to sleep, scared of the nightmares. My parents told me that one couldn't have more than one bad dream each night. I soon found out this wasn't true, so after waking from a nightmare, I would sit up in bed, willing myself to stay awake the rest of the night. I never succeeded, and would wake up in the morning lying across the bed at odd angles, having slipped from my vigil.

Givatayim

It was around 1951 when we moved to Givatayim. Our neighborhood was a place of dirt roads which turned to mud in the winter rains. In summer, the chamsin, scorching waves of heat, would come rolling in from the desert. We lived on the top floor of the tallest building in sight, a three-story apartment house next to an empty lot. Across the street was a thorny field where snakes hid in summer, waiting to pounce on any kid foolish enough to take the dare to walk across barefoot. On the other side of our building, after a few houses, the road came to an abrupt end and sprouted a community of makeshift shacks housing the Temanim, the newly arrived Yemenite immigrants.

The most important thing in Givatayim was my friends, Varda and Aviva. From the time our mothers first took turns walking us to and from kindergarten, we always played together. Most of the time we jumped rope. I was the one who first learned how, just like I was the one who figured out how to keep a ball bouncing, but soon we were all jumping rope constantly. We usually tried to get Tammi, Aviva's little sister, to turn one end so that two of us were free to jump, but she was not always willing. We did this every day, for hours. Sometimes we also played a game similar to jacks, only with pebbles, balancing a stone on the back of our hand and trying to keep it from dropping while we picked up more.

It was boring at home. I tried to get away as much as I could to play with my friends, but sometimes they took afternoon naps. One Saturday I went over to Aviva's house. Her black dog was chained on the porch. He barked and barked at me. I inched forward slowly, hoping his chain was short enough so that I could get by him to the door. I came to a spot where I realized I was stuck. If I went forward any more he could reach me, yet if I retreated there was no certainty of escape. I stood there, frozen, for what seemed like hours.

Finally the door opened and Aviva's mother came out. "Everyone's sleeping," she said, "come back later." I felt terrible for having woken her up.

I liked Aviva better than Varda, I decided one time. Varda sometimes told fibs. But we had to be careful at Aviva's house. We were all afraid of her father, who would fly into rages when he was drunk. She showed us her doll with the head recently torn off, a victim of his temper.

At my house, it was the twins we had to watch out for. My family lived on the third, and the twins lived on the ground floor. Avram and Chaiim were a year older than I, but were in my class in school. I lived in fear of them. They would attack without warning. Even their little sister, Zipora, who was two years younger than I, was a terror and was sure to break any toy I carelessly left outside. One day during recess, Avram cornered me in the classroom when we were the only ones there and kicked me viciously. Their father, everyone knew, beat them a lot.

Sometimes at home, I would try to get Hanan to play with me, but he was four years older and usually busy with schoolwork. I decided to help him. I saw on his homework page that he had forgotten to finish all the 5s, so I took a pencil and completed the numerals for him. He got very upset at what I'd done. It turned out they weren't 5s, but the letter zayin, which looks like a 5 without the top bar. I was being a pest, I knew, but what else was there for me to do?

One day Hanan brought home a stray puppy he had found. My mother made him take it out because she didn't want to take care of a dog. The next day we found out that some children had stoned it to death. That was just what some kids did.

During Purim, when we all dressed up in costumes, gangs of little masked kids roamed the neighborhood stealing costumes from other kids. I took off the pretty earrings and scarf from my gypsy costume when walking to and from school. One day my brother came home with his face all bruised. They'd attacked him and taken the little wooden sword he had so proudly made himself. He wasn't crying though, and I was very impressed by his bravery.

I too was cruel, collecting butterflies, so plentiful then, in a jar and slowly filling it up with water and watching them drown. Why did I do that? Maybe it was to see what would happen. Maybe because it was the only power allowed me, the power over smaller creatures. Maybe that's why we were cruel as kids, maybe that's why the adults, themselves powerless victims of cruelty, were cruel to us children, or were unable to love us as we needed to be loved.

When we started first grade in a new school two kilometers away, Aviva, Varda and I would walk back and forth together, imagining a giant eagle that would take us on his back to fly us wherever we wished. Yet the walk didn't tire us. As soon as we got home, we would get our rope and jump until it got dark.

One day, while I was playing with my friends in the empty lot between my house and Aviva's, I noticed Avram and Zipora watching us from a distance. I saw Zipora pick up a rock and throw it in my direction. I froze, watching it sail towards me in slow motion. I knew it would hit me, but I couldn't move. After a long time when nothing happened, I thought the rock had missed me after all, but suddenly there was a big explosion on the top of my head.

The next thing I remember is my father appearing and asking me, "Did Avram throw the rock?"

"Yes," I said, not contradicting him. Some of the other kids told me the next day that they sneaked up to Avram's apartment window in the evening and saw his father holding Avram under a table, crashing his head onto the underside of the table over and over again, while Avram screamed, "enough, enough."

I don't know why I didn't tell my father it was Zipora who

8

threw the rock. Maybe the same paralysis that had immobilized me as I stood watching the rock sail towards me had also prevented me from making the effort to correct my father's assumption, or maybe it was to get even with Avram for kicking me in school. I'm not sure why I lied, but the consequences of my falsehood haunted me with guilt.

Yet there was also love in Givatayim. There was Benni's mother, who lived in our building. I loved her smooth, honey-colored skin, her delicate perfume, her face, the most beautiful I'd ever seen, but above all I loved her baby, Benni. When my mother told me that eating honey was good for one's complexion, I said that Benni's mother must eat a lot of honey. This then became a family joke, but I was serious, for wasn't she the most perfect lady in the world? I would wait outside her door for hours, finally summoning up the courage to knock very, very softly, afraid to bother her. Yet, amazingly, Benni's mother always heard me and opened the door.

"Can I play with Benni?" I whispered, afraid to ask for so much.

"Of course, dear," she would say. "Come in."

What pleasures awaited me then! If Benni wasn't sleeping, I got to hold him in my arms, in my lap, caressing his soft skin, holding his feathery head to my cheek, touching his tiny hands and fingers. He was a soft bundle of sweet-smelling love. I watched mesmerized as he was changed, bathed, and my heart felt like bursting with happiness when his mother asked me to help.

When Benni took a nap, his mother let me look at the beautiful things in their apartment. They were from a country very different from where my family came from, someplace mysterious. Benni's mother had been a princess there, I was sure. Years later, I learned they were from Iraq. At the end of each visit, she would offer me a pretty bowl full of powdered, puffy, pastel-colored candies. I would carefully pick one of these delicate delights. It had a soft, cloudlike chewiness and tasted like a fragrant flower, filling me with contentment.

Our apartment had its own unique touches. Whoever had painted it evidently had a creative streak and had put in a daring touch by spraying flakes of reflective substance onto the walls of the front room. When the light was turned on, it would reflect off the material and hundreds of sparkling stars shone on the walls. This effect didn't last long, however, because the bits came off easily, and kids just couldn't resist peeling them. I once made the mistake of telling Hanan how much I liked one particularly large flake in a corner, which seemed to twinkle especially for me whenever I entered the room. He immediately went over to my special star and pulled it off the wall, and that was the end of that.

One day, as I was bouncing a ball on the landing between the second and third floor of our building, my mother came down the stairs from our apartment, accompanied by two of my brother's schoolmates. "Where are you going?" I asked.

"To the store," she said, walking past me. There was a little grocery store in our neighborhood.

"Will you bring me back some gum?" I asked.

My mother turned and stared back at me, not saying a word. Something about her unusually direct gaze made me remember it, even these many decades later. After a few seconds she turned and continued walking silently down the stairs.

I went out to play with Varda and Aviva. We jumped rope until it started getting dark; then their parents called them home. My mother wasn't back yet, and my father hadn't come from work either. I stayed outside, playing with my ball, until it got very dark. Aviva's mother came out and asked me where my mother was.

"She went to the store," I said.

"Come and wait for her at our house," she said.

They were having supper on the porch. They invited me to join them, but I didn't want to eat, and just sat at the side watching. They were eating salad, with tomatoes. Tomatoes always made me gag, but this evening they looked so delicious and juicy. I regretted saying I didn't want anything. Just then my parents arrived.

They said my brother was in the hospital. He had gotten a ride, together with some other kids, in a pickup truck, and had fallen or been pushed out the back while it was moving. He had a concussion and was in a coma.

For several weeks, his prognosis was uncertain. My parents told me not to say anything about it to my grandmother, as it would upset her. They told her he was visiting my aunt in Benyamina. There were times Hanan regained consciousness, but then was not in his right mind. One time, when my parents were visiting, he mistook someone's shoe for a friend's dachshund. Another time he broke through the screen of his room's window and escaped. A doctor found him hours later, wandering naked around the grounds.

Miraculously, Hanan made a complete recovery. My grandmother cried when they told her what had really happened. The relatives praised my coolness for not having told her about it, but for me, keeping secrets was just a regular part of life. I knew you kept certain things from some people, like that man my parents didn't like. When he knocked on our door, we would all be absolutely quiet, so that he'd think we weren't home and go away. Since nobody we knew had phones, visits couldn't be easily arranged ahead of time.

We ate mainly potatoes and vegetables, but I was a very picky eater and wouldn't eat any vegetables except for green beans. The only meat around was mutton, but since it was covered with flies when hanging in the marketplace, my mother wouldn't buy it, so we rarely ate meat. When we could get beef it was too tough for me to eat. Occasionally we got a chicken, a treat I loved. Because there was food rationing, chicken was hard to come by. My father would smuggle one home in the hollow spaces of the car whenever we went to visit our grandmother after she moved to live near my Aunt Herta and Uncle Fritz, who kept chickens. They lived in the little village of Benyamina, just 50 kilometers to the north, but the trip took many hours because every few kilometers one of the ancient tires of the old Renault would have a flat.

"Puncture," my brother and I would yell, and we'd all get out and wait by the side of the road while my father, sweating profusely, changed the tire. It was impossible to get any car parts or new tires, so the old ones were patched over and over again. The car eventually broke down completely and we never got another one, but while we had it my father would always hide a chicken in the hollow walls for the trip back from Benyamina.

Our food was also supplemented by what we received in packages from our relatives in America. These boxes contained an assortment of odd things, including the strangest clothes. One time there was a red shirt for my brother, which of course he could never wear, since red was a girl's color. Another time there were two matching shirts, one for me and one for Hanan, made of some shiny material in rectangles of many different bright colors. We could never be seen in such garish clowns' costumes, so these too were a waste. What was even weirder than the clothes was the American food. It was also brightly colored and shiny, and was called Jello. It seemed more like entertainment than food. From these various items we came to the logical conclusion that Americans, though well-meaning and rich, were crazy.

There was one item, however, which redeemed these otherwise senseless people. It was that most delicious substance, powdered milk. My mother would put spoonfuls of the precious stuff in my tea, with me always begging for more. Regular milk made me gag and I just couldn't drink it, but this stuff was heavenly. I would manage to climb up to the highest shelf of the tallest cupboard to sneak a spoonful to eat straight from the can, savoring its silken texture. This was not the grainy instant kind of today, but the finely powdered tinned variety of long ago.

My Addiction

Like zillions of other little kids the world over, I sucked my thumb. Only I didn't stop until I was eleven years old. I only sucked my right thumb. I tried the other one but found it completely useless. It lacked some mysterious ingredient essential for thumbsucking. My right thumb, on the other hand, was just perfect. How to describe the feeling of thumbsucking? How does a junkie describe the pleasure of his fix? To put it simply, it made everything OK. All my troubles would melt away, magically replaced by a heavenly contentment.

My right thumb had developed a distinctive callus from where it rested on my lower front teeth. This mark was what enabled me to distinguish right from left. I wondered how kids who didn't suck their thumb got by without this aid.

When I was about to start kindergarten, my parents told me that thumbsucking was not allowed in school. This was a shock, for I had never before been expected to submit to such a state of deprivation. However, I was determined to overcome this challenge. Through constant, diligent effort, I managed to subdue my need while I was in school. Aware now of the shame associated with this activity, I also refrained when I was with my two new friends, Varda and Aviva. Sometimes, however, my thumb, of its own accord, managed to find its way into my mouth while I was distracted and had let my guard down for a moment. I would then quickly slide it out and pretend that I had been scratching my chin or chewing my thumbnail.

One day, on one of those rare occasions when my father's car was up and running, he and my mother gave Varda, Aviva, Aviva's mother, and me a ride home from school. Since the car was crowded, Aviva had to sit on her mother's lap.

"Aviva's a baby, sitting on her mommy's lap," I teased her.

"Not as big a baby as you are," retorted my mother. "You still suck your thumb."

There was a shocked silence. My secret was out. The humiliation was unbearable.

"It's just when I go to sleep," I whimpered. Surely, I thought, that was acceptable.

"Other times too," my mother insisted.

Of course this was true. My thumb went into my mouth the minute I got home and spent much of its time there, but did everyone have to know this?

"It's just when I'm in bed, just to go to sleep," I kept telling Varda and Aviva the next day. I knew other kids had special blankets and rituals at night. Surely it was OK to be a baby at bedtime. This seemed to satisfy my friends, or maybe they were just tired of listening to my excuses. Anyway, the topic was not mentioned again.

My parents also didn't bother me about my thumbsucking as I grew older. Maybe they realized that I needed this comfort through the turmoil of the coming years, as we left Israel for Germany when I was eight, and then Germany for the US when I was nine. Although I learned German and then English very quickly, I couldn't make friends in these new countries. I just clung to my trusted old companion, my thumb, until puberty replaced this first love with other yearnings. My thumb then gradually lost its magic power, and eventually the callus faded away.

15

My Early Education

I had two major illnesses in Israel in the early 1950s, scarlet fever and diphtheria. These two events, coming close together in time, are mixed up in my memory so that I cannot tell which memory goes with which disease.

I remember a day, just a few weeks after I started first grade, when I felt chilly. It was recess, and I decided to stay in the classroom, where it was warmer.

"Why aren't you outside?" the teacher asked, surprised, for I usually could hardly wait to climb to the top of the monkey bars and hang upside down.

"I'm cold," I said.

An older child was recruited to walk me home. It had rained the night before, and the dirt road and fields we had to cross were a sea of mud. I was luckier than most of the kids, for my father worked for a wholesale rubber rainwear company, so I had boots and a raincoat, but as I trudged the long way, I thought I could not bear the cold.

"I'm cold," I said to my mother when I finally reached home. She put me to bed.

I have a memory of my throat feeling like it was being squeezed, and the air making a whistling sound as I breathed, and feeling scared, and my parents telling me to lie down and stay very quiet. For years afterwards I could feel the squeezing in my throat whenever I got "overly excited," as my parents called it.

It was evening and a doctor was at my home. He and my mother went into the kitchen. After a while I heard a little "ding." The doctor and my mother came out of the kitchen and over to my bed. Suddenly the doctor was giving me a shot! I was too surprised to react. He placed a little empty vial in my hand. It was wonderfully warm. The doctor and my mother went to the kitchen again. Again I heard the chime. This time I was ready. I clenched my butt muscles so the needle wouldn't hurt going in. Again I comforted myself with the warmth of a new vial. This went on several times more.

"This is the last one," the doctor told me, but afterwards I heard the bell again. After the fifth shot, deciding to save its delicious heat for later, I placed this new vial next to the cooled ones on the shelf over my bed. On the sixth shot, the doctor had trouble getting the needle in, my butt was so tense. "Relax your muscles," he said. "This is the last shot." I didn't believe him. I thought it would go on forever, and broke down crying. Then, to my surprise, he really was leaving, and I placed the final vial next to the other warm one.

The next morning, I reached for the two warm vials. To my surprise, they were both as cold as the first ones whose heat I had enjoyed the night before. Thus I got one of my first science lessons: Heat dissipates into the air; and two early life lessons: Don't put off enjoyment till later, and you can't always trust doctors.

I was sick for a long time. My brother was sent away to my aunt and grandmother's place in Benyamina so he wouldn't catch what I had. Now I had nobody to annoy. Varda and Aviva couldn't visit me. Of course there was no TV or even a radio. I had only a couple of toys, but my two dolls were a comfort, and I played with the little vials from the six shots of the first night and the ones I received from the nurse who came daily for the next week, giving me a single shot each day. I lined the vials up on my sheet and played pretend games with them. But it wasn't enough to ward off the unbearable boredom that engulfed me. After I was not quite so sick and in the slow recovery stage, my mother went back to work. She worked in the same wholesale warehouse as my father.

"How long will you be gone?" I asked, terrified of the infinite emptiness ahead.

She took a small clock and placed it on my bed. She showed me where the long arm and the short arm would be when she would return. I kept my gaze on the clock, and after some time I noticed that the long arm was moving very slowly around. But the short arm still seemed to stay in the same place. I fell asleep, and when I woke up I saw that the short arm had also changed position. It was now closer to the time my mother would come home. And thus I tamed the hours and bound them to the movements of the clock, and time lost some of its frightening power.

Still, there were all those long hours with nothing to do. How I yearned for relief from this depressing desolation. One day my parents brought me a book from the library but were too busy to read it to me. In the morning they left it on my bed so I could look at the pictures. I opened it, but was disappointed because the illustrations were small and uncolored. It was mostly words. I didn't know how to read, but in the few weeks I had spent in school before I got sick we had gone through the alphabet and learned a few words. I knew how to write and read my name, and "shalom," and "school." I had also learned the "dots," the Hebrew vowel sounds which are marks placed along the letters and are used in children's books to make it easier to sound out the words. I tried to sound out the words of the title. They were strange, difficult words, but after a long time I had the title: *The Brave Little Rabbit*. Curious about this rabbit and what there was to be brave about, I tackled the story.

She was the smallest, youngest in a family who lived in a burrow, and the descriptions of this cute rabbit were so real, and the games she played with her brothers and sisters seemed just like the games I used to play with my friends before I got sick, so I wanted to know more about them, and kept on sounding out those words until after a while they lost some of their hard edges. Then there came this animal called a "w. e. a. s. e. l," which I'd never heard of before, but who was really mean and was trying to eat all the rabbits. Now I really had to find out what happened to them! This w e a s e l was really

18

nasty and things looked quite hopeless for the rabbits. Only, the little rabbit was not just brave, she was also clever. I was so excited that I didn't notice that I wasn't sounding out the words any more, that the letters were just melting into one another by themselves. The little rabbit hatched an ingenious plan to outwit that evil weasel. Now I was coasting along the sentences, which, it turned out, were really quite smooth, and so I slipped off them and started gliding effortlessly with the rabbits and the weasel. I was with the little rabbit when she performed her courageous feat and outsmarted that weasel. I saw him slink off in defeat, banished, never to bother the rabbits again. But the most amazing thing was that I found I had reached the end of the book!

When my parents came home, I first asked "What's a weasel?" and then I asked them to bring me more library books, which they did eventually, and which I devoured hungrily. I was out of school for several months. When I finally returned in the spring, I was surprised that the other kids in my class were still painfully sounding out the words when they read, while I soared in my newfound freedom.

Uma

I called her "Uma," a mispronunciation of Oma, the German word for grandmother. Her real name, though, was Lina. I knew her as a big, gray, shapeless woman wearing baggy, shapeless dresses and trudging heavily on thick, stumpy legs. "Old-lady legs," the kids used to call them. She used to sigh and complain about the heat. I remember the excitement of her visits. Hanan and I used to race each other for the special chair, which we carried down the stairs and put on the first landing. She would rest there a few minutes from her climb, then continue on up, while we carried the chair to the second landing. She'd sit down again to catch her breath, then finally continue to our third floor apartment.

She was a widow. Her husband had died many years before as a German soldier in World War I, leaving her with two small children, a six-year-old girl and my infant father. In the 1930s she and her two children emigrated to Palestine in time to avoid the fate of many others, including my mother's parents, who were killed in the Holocaust. Thus she was the only grandparent I had.

She lived near us at first, but eventually moved to the small village of Benyamina, in the north of Israel, where her daughter Herta and son-in-law Fritz lived. It was a peaceful little place of dusty fields and clucking chickens, and I used to love the times my parents would let me stay there for an extended visit. Uma and I would play checkers together on the table with the bright crocheted tablecloth. She had never learned to speak Hebrew well and so spoke German to me. She would take out a little slate and some chalk and I would practice writing my name in German, over and over again, struggling with the strange angles of the old-world script.

One day stands out in my memory. My grandmother took out a big, heavy book and opened it on the table in front of us.

There before me were the most precious sights I had ever seen. They were cards, hundreds of them, each one more beautiful than the last. There were paintings of ships and flowers and queens and princes, with lovely ladies in fashionable costumes from exotic countries. They were luxurious to touch, with silk and satin and fur fabrics on the ladies' dresses, and soft feathers on the birds. Some were edged in gold and some had silver glitter. My favorite one had peacock feathers. These were cards her future husband had sent when he was courting her. There were so many; it was such a big album. I figured he must have sent her one every day, knowing how much pleasure they gave.

At one point a photograph fell out of the book. I saw a lovely woman with thick and shiny hair, standing tall and slender, smiling a dimpled smile. There was something vaguely familiar about her.

"Who is that?" I asked.

"That was me," my grandmother replied.

I gasped. "You were beautiful, Uma."

"Yes," she said softly.

This was such a surprise to me, to realize that my shapeless grandmother, with the coarse hairs on her chin, could have been this pretty, graceful woman with the sweet smile.

Whenever I came to visit I would ask to see the book, and I never tired of looking at its lovely contents.

When I was eight, my parents and I left Israel. It would be many years before I would see my grandmother again, though my parents kept in touch with the family in Israel by mail. From the way my mother complained about Lina, I gathered that my parents did not altogether approve of her. She was too selfish and irresponsible, and now she was becoming absentminded and somewhat "senile," my mother said, though she seemed as strong-willed as ever.

When I was 22 I traveled back to Israel and saw my grandmother again. Now it was she who was surprised at the transformation, for I was no longer the little girl she had last seen. I felt both of our excitement, yet found myself at a loss for words. Then she announced, "You have a boyfriend, yes?"

I was surprised. The fact that I was living and traveling with a guy to whom I wasn't married was something that everyone else in my family pretended wasn't happening.

"That's wonderful!" She continued breathlessly. "Love is the most important thing. Money doesn't matter; love is the only thing that counts."

I told her we were going to hitchhike through Africa, and she was as happy and excited about it as I was. Although I never saw my grandmother again, for she died in 1973 before I could revisit Israel, I think of her as a kindred spirit.

Leaving

There were odd things going on at home.

One day I found Ima stuffing sewing supplies into a plastic food bowl that had come in one of the packages from America.

"Why are you putting the threads in there?" I asked.

"I'm going to give the bowl to Herta," my mother said, "and I thought she would like some sewing things too."

I was surprised. "But that's your bowl for keeping leftovers."

"I want to give it to Aunt Herta for her birthday," my mother explained.

I thought it was a peculiar birthday present, but since I didn't really care about it, went off to play.

Some days later, I was in my father's workplace, a basement warehouse office in Tel-Aviv. We were all there, my mother, father, and brother. Suddenly I saw the little miniature cupboard that had been made for my grandmother when she was a little girl, and which now was my favorite plaything. It had tiny, perfectly made working doors and drawers. What was it doing in my father's office? And why was my mother putting little things in the drawers? My heart sank.

"Are you going to give this to Herta too?" I wailed.

My mother stopped and looked at my father. The game was up. He told me, then.

We were going to go to Germany, then America in a couple of weeks. It had to be a secret, because my father was still in the army reserves, where he had to serve one month each year until he was 45. I mustn't tell any of my friends that we were leaving. They were packing the things we were going to take with us. We couldn't take much, because we were officially only going for a three-week vacation, so were only taking our favorite things. We were there today to get some new shoes, because they were cheaper here than where we were going. I would get two new pairs of shoes that day, but couldn't tell anyone, because getting two pairs of shoes at one time was unheard of and would arouse suspicion. My parents knew I could keep my mouth shut, like that time my brother had been in the hospital in a coma, and I had not told my grandmother.

At this point I was in a state of amazed shock. America! We were going to that place where everyone was rich!

Then I remembered the weird American clothes.

"Can I take my ruffled dress?" I asked. "And can I wear my soft yellow shirt and plaid skirt on the train, er, plane?" I stumbled on, realizing suddenly that we were going to fly in an airplane.

My parents reassured me that I could take my favorite clothes, as well as my newest doll. However, my father told me sternly, girls with long hair were not allowed on the plane.

I realized that this was a ploy to get me to consent to a haircut, which was a constant bone of contention between my mother and me. She liked my hair really, really short, "mid-ear" she would tell the barber, "and use the electric clippers on the back of her neck." All this, I felt, made my head look like someone's naked bottom. I had just managed to get it to a decent length, and had dreams of a ponytail some day. Still, I had just been offered a trip in an airplane and a fantastic new life, so was willing to concede on matters of vanity. I agreed to get my hair cut, not realizing that for decades to come my father would gloat at how I had been duped.

I asked another question. "Is there going to be war in America?"

War was something I feared. In school we had memorized a poem about the bad, bad Arabs. I had also heard my brother and his friends, who were in seventh grade, talking excitedly about a film they had seen in class which showed Israeli soldiers lying dead but with their eyes open, because, as the boys explained, "They still want to keep on fighting for our country."

"No," my father said, giving me an odd look, "there's no danger of war in America."

"But there's Russia," Hanan insisted.

"There's not going to be a war," my father repeated, and the matter was settled.

The day came when we said goodbye to our relatives: Uma, Herta, Fritz, my mother's brother Siegmund, his wife Betty, and their little son Ami. Everyone cried, even Uncle Fritz with the fierce mustache. On the last night, I put my few remaining possessions in a shoebox and, together with a letter, gave it to one of our relatives to deliver to Varda and Aviva after we were gone.

The morning we left, I was bundled into three pairs of underwear, a pair of thick pants, two shirts, a skirt, a long-sleeved dress, two sweaters, and a coat over it all. Clothes were cheaper in Israel. I complained about being hot and itchy, but my mother told me that it would be very cold in Germany, and I comforted myself with visions of playing in the snow. We got a ride to the airport. There was a mosquito buzzing in the car. "Say goodbye to the last Israeli mosquito you'll see," someone said. I clutched my doll, so glad she was going with me.

"Say goodbye to your country," my mother said. I looked out the plane window just in time to see a strip of beige beach disappear into a blue sea, then blue sky, then white clouds.

There was snow on the ground when we landed in Switzerland. I had imagined snow would be soft, but it made hard crunchy sounds when I walked on it. I didn't feel good, and cried. I didn't recognize the feeling I had, didn't know it was bitter cold, so different from cold I had known in Israel. It was February 1956, with record cold temperatures in Europe.

We stayed at a hotel. I was given a shiny red apple. Apples were rare in Israel, and I had looked forward to being in a place where there were lots of them. But the apple was mealy and I didn't like it. I had some gum from the plane, and when I woke up in the morning, the gum was in my hair. It took a long time to get it out. My father also had his disappointments. He told us that it was customary to put one's shoes outside the door, and the hotel staff would clean and shine them overnight. We put our shoes out, but in the morning they were still dirty. I guess things had changed since my father had been there.

We went to a department store, and I experienced my first escalator ride. I felt awed and overwhelmed by all the things for sale. The next day, or maybe it was the day after, we took the train to Germany.

New School

It was my first day in the German school. When I entered the building with my parents, a bunch of girls, seeing a new student, raced towards us. "Are you Catholic or Protestant?" they asked breathlessly.

"Noemi is Jewish," my father said. Their perplexed faces told me that they didn't know what to make of this. I didn't know what to make of it either, for I had never heard of the existence of Christianity.

The morning had been a blur. Was it the blur that comes from looking at a memory after many years, or the blur of too many images in too short a time, for I was still in the first weeks of adjusting to this new country? Maybe it was the blur of just following my parents obediently, not knowing what I felt.

Then a sharp jolt brought everything into clear focus. I saw something so strange that it changed everything. I saw Hanan crying. My big brother, who never cried! Even the time that he'd gotten beat up by a gang of boys who stole his wooden sword, there had been no tears on his bruised face. Now, however, he was weeping as our parents left him in front of his classroom, and I woke up to the horror of my situation. For surely it must be terrible if Hanan was crying. So I let loose, and wailed, and sobbed. But it was no use, my parents left, and there I was, in a strange classroom.

I was just starting to learn German. So, that first day, I didn't really understand what the teacher was saying, but sensed that she was making a well-intentioned fuss over me. I also realized that I was in a very different culture, for my mother had spent a long time teaching me how to do a proper "Knicks," the curtsy which German girls were expected to do when meeting grownups. I was introduced to the class, which was all girls, for German public schools had separate classes for the boys. I was led to my desk. From the teacher's gestures I figured out that I was supposed to sit with my hands folded together on top of the desk. Since that was the only instruction I understood, I followed it to the letter, and from then on always sat with my hands carefully clasped on my desk. This led the teacher to conclude that I was a model student, and thus she never gave me any trouble.

The most notable thing about the classroom were the paintings which ringed the upper walls. These were very strange pictures. They all involved some form of torture. One painting showed several men in some kind of uniform or costume whipping another man, who was stripped to his waist. The whips had little sharp-pointed knobs at the tips and the man had red bleeding marks on his back. Another painting showed them putting a leafless wreath on his head, with blood dripping onto his face from the points where thorns in the wreath pierced his skin. Another picture showed the man tied to a piece of wood, with the other men hammering nails into his hands. I was fascinated by these paintings, had never seen anything like them. There was something darkly compelling about their gory sensuality. However, I sensed that it would be wrong to stare at them, so wound up taking furtive glances at these titillating pictures throughout the day.

I also looked at the other girls, and enviously admired their pretty dresses, the skirts puffy with multiple starched petticoats. Later, the teacher had to leave the classroom for a few minutes. What an amazing change came over the class the instant she was gone. The prim little Fräuleins leaped onto the tops of their desks, jumping, shrieking, yelling and throwing books and pens across the room. This too was a new one for me. I had been used to the informal Israeli school, where teachers were called by their first name, where you could sit any way you wanted and where there didn't seem to be such a need to go crazy when the teacher was out of sight.

In the yard at recess the girls descended on me with

countless questions, which I didn't know how to answer. I felt like an animal in a zoo. Someone kindly gave me an apple. I tried to eat it, but found I could not swallow. I couldn't move, either. I didn't know what to do. I had always been an active kid in Israel, running, doing flips on the bars, jumping rope for hours, playing all kinds of games, but here I didn't know what to do except sit with my hands folded on my desk.

A Cold Time

In the year that we spent in Germany, my parents went through the legal process of getting reparation money from the German government for my mother's parents, who had been killed by the Nazis. Although my brother had apparently been told about this history when we were still in Israel, I knew nothing about Nazis or what had happened to my maternal grandparents. I just went to school and learned to read and write the language to perfection, and to speak it with only a slight accent. I also learned to feel awkward, ugly, and inhibited in my cheap clothes and crude foreign ways. In Israel, where everyone had so little, I felt privileged because I had a few toys. Here, I was among kids who had so much more than I did, and I was miserable. One day my parents announced they would buy me a new dress, and I got my hopes up. Maybe I would get to be like the other girls in my class, with their frilly dresses and layers of puffy petticoats. Sadly, the new dress they bought, with its single limp slip, was a drab disappointment, and I felt as inadequate as ever in the outfit my parents considered extravagant.

My parents got jobs at the US Air Force base in Wiesbaden, for having lived under British rule in Palestine for many years, they could both speak English. My mother had learned it already in school in Germany, and my father had taken a course in Palestine. We first rented two rooms in a big house owned by the mother of one of their young coworkers, Charlotte, who also lived there. I remember Charlotte as being very pretty and kind, letting me play with her stuffed animals and accompanying us to the zoo. However, we wound up moving after a few weeks. After my father died, I asked my mother about it. She told me that Charlotte had accused my father of coming to her room at night and trying to seduce her. "Aba and I decided that it was wishful thinking on her part, for after all she was an old maid," said my mother, "so we figured it was best to break off the friendship."

"You believed him?" I asked.

"Oh yes," said my mother. "Aba said he wasn't attracted to her at all. After all, she was an old maid."

"But wasn't she quite a bit younger than you?"

"Yes, she was younger, but she was an old maid. It was probably wishful thinking on her part," repeated my mother.

So we had moved to a small attic apartment. In order to save money on furniture, Hanan and I slept on vinyl folding lawn loungers, in the bathroom. It was unheated, and that winter was a terribly cold one in Europe. We were warm enough, however, for my parents had invested in that wonderful German staple, eiderdown comforters. Every morning I was awakened to the buzzing of my father's electric razor as he shaved at the sink next to me, his breath forming clouds. "Go back to sleep," he would say, "it's too early for you to get up for school." But I wasn't able to sleep with the buzzing and the radio he always had on blaring the news.

It never occurred to me to speak up if something bothered me. My feelings were silly. This was a fundamental part of my life, like the air I breathed, and I never questioned it. If my parents noticed that I was unhappy or my feelings were hurt, they called me a "Beleidigte Leberwurst," which translates literally to "offended liverwurst," a ridiculous figure. It was also unthinkable for me to have an opinion contrary to my parents'. A stern "NE-O-MI" from my father was enough to bring me back into line. I learned at an early age never to show my feelings or express my opinions to my parents, to be a "good" girl without needs. I remember one day when we were at some kind of fair. There was a stand selling gingerbread hearts. We passed several groups of children, all of them proudly wearing, on ribbons around their necks, huge hearts beautifully decorated with colored icing. I walked on ahead so that my parents wouldn't see my tears. Suddenly, I heard my

31

mother ask me, "Do you want a heart?" My hopes went up, but the heart I got was a tiny plain one.

The habits of hiding my feelings came to encompass my relations with others also, and it took decades for me to overcome these early lessons. Most of the time I retreated into myself, playing pretend games or daydreaming. My inner world became my sanctuary, and I found happiness in my fantasy life. Other times I would get sick. I remember the night I woke up with a bad earache, and my crying woke Hanan. "Lie on your other side and go back to sleep," he told me. I tried but couldn't, for the pain was excruciating. When morning finally came and I could tell my mother, she took me to a doctor. He gave me medicine and put a heat lamp next to my ear, and its soothing warmth felt wonderful.

"She needs a hat for the cold weather," the doctor said.

Ima bought me a red knitted hat with ear flaps, and I loved its comfortable warmth in the snowy weather.

My parents hired a woman to take care of me after school. Her name was Frau Teuer. Years later I learned that she was one of the few Germans who admitted to my parents that they had been Nazis during the war. She had to belong to the Nazi Party, she explained, in order to get the necessary permit to open a home for war orphans, but she hadn't realized what was happening. My parents trusted her because unlike most Germans who claimed complete innocence, she was honest. Having no knowledge of Nazis or German history, I was unaware of all this at the time. Frau Teuer was kind to me and I liked her. I liked to draw at her house, sketching the vases of flowers she always had on her dining room table, and she was happy with the pictures I gave her. Her husband made me uneasy, however. He liked to talk about spanking naughty little girls.

One day some of my classmates came over to play at my home. Suddenly, a loud fart escaped me. The girls giggled. I was mortified, for I was sure German girls never farted.

I wrote Aviva and Varda, and they wrote me back. We decorated our letters with borders of colored-pencil flowers and called each other the nonsense nicknames we had made up in Israel, trying desperately to hold on to what had been, but it was futile. I had left their world far behind. It was the same when my parents tried to get me to write my relatives in Israel. I just stared at the paper, unable to think of anything to say out of the emptiness inside me. This new place, with its big stores full of beautiful things and the doll-like girls in fancy dresses, seemed far superior to my old life. Having come from such a shabby place, I felt worthless.

My parents decided to take a two-week trip to Italy during the Christmas holidays. They took my thirteen-year-old brother with them, but since I was only nine, left me at a "Kinderheim," an orphanage which also took in children on a temporary basis. I think there were about 20 kids there. My cousin Raffi, who was two years younger than I, was also staying there because his mother was ill. The place was in the middle of the woods, and the nuns taking care of us kids were kind enough. I spent most of the time taking care of the baby doll that my parents had given me for my ninth birthday. I named her Schätzchen, which means little treasure or darling, and kept her in a cardboard box which I dragged around on a string behind me wherever I went.

Once a week we got a bath. The sisters put some warm water in the bathtub, and each girl in line took her turn sitting in the tub while the nuns washed her. The water was pretty dirty by the time I got in, for it wasn't changed until all the girls were finished and it was the boys' turn. I said that there was still soap on me when I got out, hoping that it would be rinsed off, but the nun just wiped it off with the towel and called the next girl. I was content there, however, playing out in the snow and with my baby doll. For Christmas, I was happy to get a new set of doll clothes, which I knew my parents had left for me. When my parents came back from

Italy, they brought me a music box which played "O Sole Mio," and a set of tiny glass ducklings, which I loved and played with for many years.

There were times that my brother had to take care of me. He would take me to a playground. One time we were on a metal spinner and a bunch of bigger kids came along and started turning it faster and faster. I wanted to get off, but they wouldn't let it slow down. Hanan leaped off. "Jump," he yelled, but I was too scared. Then it was spinning so fast I couldn't stand it, so finally I jumped blindly. I somehow fell partly under the platform, which hit my head. Hanan pulled me out and laid me on a bench. After a while I felt OK. "Don't tell Ima and Aba," he said.

Coming to America

The only thing that I remember of the flight to the US is that my hair was now long enough for a ponytail, though barely, and only with the help of several bobby pins.

We stayed with our relatives in Baltimore for a few days, then flew for a short stay with my mother's relatives in Chicago. They had two daughters, slightly older than I. My parents thought they should arrive with presents, and bought each of them a Barbie doll. When we arrived, I saw that the girls had a closetful, not only of the most clothes I had ever seen in one place, but also several Barbie dolls and their many outfits. I longed to have a doll with such beautiful hair and clothes to play with, but as usual, kept my feelings to myself.

We then flew to Portland, Oregon, and stayed with my father's cousin Hedwig and her family. She was a kind lady who immediately decided that I was too skinny and needed fattening up. I watched in amazement as Hedwig prepared scrambled eggs for me using almost a whole stick of butter.

All I remember of my first day of school was getting lost on the way home, and running, panicked, through unfamiliar streets for what seemed like hours. People along the way asked if I needed help, but I didn't know how to explain my situation in English, so just kept running. In the last weeks in Germany, I had learned a little English from American comic books and a little book called *English Through Pictures*, but I was still too scared to speak it. Finally, I happened to stumble upon the row of familiar pansies lining the walkway to my aunt's house.

It was the middle of the school year, and I was placed into third grade, where I had been when I left Israel a year earlier. Because the German school year started in the spring, I had spent a whole year in third grade there, and so wound up spending a total of two years in third grade. After a couple of months in Portland, however, I was reading with the advanced group, and ahead in all my subjects, so I was allowed to skip fourth grade for the coming school year. Academically, the German school had been inferior to the Israeli school, with the American school even more behind than the German. Socially, however, the American kids were way ahead, and I was completely lost in that subject.

After having learned to understand the written word in three languages so rapidly, you might expect that I was a linguistic prodigy who could navigate the spoken word just as easily. Unfortunately, the opposite was the case. Although I learned how to read and write German and English, each in a few weeks, it took me over a decade to begin to learn how to talk to people. The sad fact was that the cultural differences completely overwhelmed me, and as much as I admired, envied and tried to imitate them, I didn't know how to talk to the strange creatures who were now my classmates. In the German school, the spotless, petticoated sweetness of the other girls had left me feeling too crude and awkward to talk. In the US, the glib banter and verbal swordplay of these socially adept American youngsters left me completely tongue-tied, unable to think of the required sophisticated responses until hours later.

It wouldn't be until my junior year in college that another social misfit would jar me out of my isolation.

I still exchanged letters with Aviva and Varda, but the distance now was insurmountable. I was much too confused to explain myself or this world to them, and eventually the letters stopped. In school I was asked to describe what Israel was like. "The houses have flat roofs," was all I could think to say.

We moved to an apartment. A most wonderful day came when my parents gave me a bicycle for my tenth birthday. Hanan took me to the parking lot and held it while I climbed on. He ran along, then let go, and after a few shaky moments, I was off flying, caught in a glorious feeling of freedom as I soared, learning to lean into turns, swerving and gliding in complete control now. I will never forget the joy of my first bike ride.

My father was a traveling salesman for a uniform company owned by his second cousin Fred, whose father had sponsored our affidavit to come to the US. Aba would be gone for weeks, driving all over the Northwest selling hospital, restaurant, and school uniforms. During the summer he would sometimes take us all with him on one of his trips. I loved the rugged scenery, but not the boredom of waiting in a hot car for hours while he conducted business. Occasionally, our parents would splurge on the special treat of staying in a motel with a swimming pool. That made up for everything.

One summer, my parents left me with my father's cousin Heini, his wife Esther, and their son Raffi, while they and my brother went on a sales trip for several weeks. Heini's family had also moved to Portland from Israel via Germany. I had a good time playing with Raffi and learning to rollerskate. Then I came down with whooping cough, and Esther very kindly took care of me. As usual, I bounced right back from being sick.

We had many relatives in Portland, for several of my father's cousins and their families had come to live there. Another of Aba's cousins was Manfred, with his wife Rachel and son Jack. Jack was a reporter for the *Oregonian*, later becoming a Pulitzer-Prize winning editor at *The New York Times*. Rachel was originally from Lithuania. My parents put her down for being too strong-willed and "wearing the pants" in her household, for they found it shocking that her husband did the dishes sometimes. Outwardly, however, none of this was revealed, and they were always polite to her.

My parents didn't want me to forget my native tongue, so sent me to Hebrew school. I remember the shock of my first day there, hearing the teacher utter the most absurd sounds imaginable, and the kids dutifully repeating them. It was a butchered form of Hebrew I had never heard before. All the "ah" sounds were turned into "oy" sounds, with each "t" pronounced like an "s," and with an intonation that to my ears sounded worse than the proverbial fingernails scraping the blackboard. It was Ashkenazi, spoken in religious services such as the Bar Mitzvahs for which most of the students were preparing, and not the Sephardic Hebrew spoken in Israel. It sounded wrong and fake to me, and I couldn't stand it.

So my brother was recruited to give me Hebrew lessons at home instead. A textbook was procured from somewhere. It was about the Zionists who had founded the first kibbutzim in Israel, and was incredibly boring, going on endlessly about the "brave pioneers." Now, the Hebrew word for pioneers is "chalutzim," which sounds similar to "chatzilim," eggplants. I had to read aloud, so to liven things up, I started substituting "brave eggplants," every time I came across "brave pioneers." This made the book more entertaining, but Hanan got annoyed and complained to our parents. The Hebrew lessons stopped then and I gradually forgot my native tongue.

We moved to a suburb, Cedar Hills, to a ranch house my parents bought. There was a big lawn, and a sweet baby next door named Mikey, for whom I was soon babysitting. There were fruit trees along the way to school, and I loved how in early spring the blossoms would shower a pink carpet of petals onto the sidewalks. Once, a classmate named Tina came over to my house after school. All I could think of doing together was to play jacks, similar to the pebble game I played with Varda and Aviva in Israel. I kept winning, and I think Tina got bored. Anyway, she didn't come again. My mother got a job in a bookstore, and would bring me books which I would read and then return. I devoured all the Nancy Drew stories. I didn't have friends, but I was pretty content, reading, watching TV, and daydreaming.

I remember sitting on the couch watching TV one evening. A show came on showing footage of a concentration camp just after it was liberated, with gaunt people staring with haunted eyes, then piles of naked bony corpses, and then a lampshade made of human skin. I looked away. "Yes," my mother said, "don't look." By that time I was aware that my mother's parents had been killed by the Nazis, but didn't know any more of the story. As it was unthinkable for me to approach my mother on any subject that might disturb her, I put it out of my mind.

In my daydreams, I could fly and travel back in time. I loved to make up stories from TV programs set in the past, and fly there to rescue people, particularly cute boys. I remember one show called "Swamp Fox," about the Revolutionary War. The hero's teenage son was mortally wounded and died on the show, but after I flew him to a cave and spent many weeks nursing him back to health, he recovered.

I started junior high, and developed a crush on this boy named Pat. Of course, there was no romantic hope for me, but I could dream. I started having trouble seeing the blackboard, so I wound up getting glasses. I remember the shock of my first day wearing them to school, when I saw that Pat had pimples and wasn't nearly as good-looking as he had been before I wore glasses.

I still liked to draw, but was uncertain and shy about my abilities. I used to draw secretly, not showing the results to anyone. One time, my father walked into my room without knocking, just as I was copying a picture from a magazine. It was a Breck Shampoo ad, and I was attempting to draw the hair just as it appeared in the picture. I had been busy concentrating on this detailed task and was unprepared for the intrusion. Caught by surprise, I quickly turned the paper over.

"What are you doing?" he asked suspiciously.

"Just drawing," I answered.

"Show it to me!" He demanded.

"No," I said, too embarrassed to show my work and holding on to it tightly.

This infuriated him. "Give it to me!" He yelled, grabbing

39

the drawing and ripping it out of my hands. He looked at it, then stomped out of my room.

"What was it?" I heard my mother ask.

"The head of a woman," My father said disgustedly. I felt he had expected to catch me drawing something sexual, and was disappointed that he hadn't. Another time, as I was in the bathroom applying nail polish to my toenails, my first foray into cosmetics, my father walked in. "When I was young, only prostitutes did that," he announced.

It was around this time that I started feeling uncomfortable around my father. My father noticed my withdrawal, and acted hurt. I knew that hurting my father made me a bad daughter, but I couldn't help my feelings.

Hanan got a scholarship to a small private high school. He didn't want to go at first, saying he wanted to stay in public school, but the family thought it would offer him a better chance to get into a good college, and so he went there. In the summer, he got into a technical program for gifted students.

My parents gave my brother a pet parakeet. He got a mate for it, and a nesting box. One day, when our parents were out, he found an egg in the box. He got terribly excited then, and kept jumping up and down all over the house, running and screaming hysterically, "An egg, an egg, an egg!" over and over, for a long time. His behavior was so strange; it seemed to me that there was something wrong with him. It worried me, but I kept it to myself.

When we were kids, Hanan and I fought every chance we got. Maybe because our parents were off-limits to us, we had to take it out on each other. It was a matter of pride for me to fight him, for it was my one chance to be in a role other than the compliant one expected of me. Before I started school myself, I had tried to pry his attention away from his schoolwork and so became a pest, a role that stuck. As we grew older he grew too busy with his schoolwork to bother fighting me, and grew distant instead. As my brother showed talent in science and math, our parents started kidding him about winning the Nobel prize one day. Only on some level, I think this wasn't a joke. He had an obligation to make our parents happy by being spectacular. As for me, I also excelled in school, but being a girl, I wasn't subjected to either encouragement or high academic expectations. I was glad, because I knew I didn't want to be like Hanan, for his seemed a dreary path.

LA Summer

After I finished seventh grade, my father was assigned to work at the Los Angeles branch of the uniform company for the summer. He decided to take the whole family with him, and we drove from our home in Portland, Oregon, to LA. My mother and brother also worked at the warehouse. We stayed in an old, rundown hotel in an industrial area. I had nothing to do in the hotel while my parents and brother were working, and was bored senseless.

One day, my brother stayed home also, for a reason I have long since forgotten. Our hotel room consisted of two spaces divided by a sliding door, painted a dull green. Suddenly, Hanan went over to the partition and said, "I bet I can punch a hole through this door." Before I could say anything, his fist crashed right through. We looked in amazement at the green-painted shards on the floor. We had both assumed that the door was made of wood, but apparently the panes were of glass, painted green to look like wood. Luckily, my brother had not been cut.

When my parents came home, they were furious and lectured us on our irresponsible behavior, pointing out that Hanan could have been seriously injured. "What would you have done if he was bleeding badly?" my father yelled at me.

I knew what to do to stop bleeding. I had just finished a first aid course in school. "I would have put pressure on it," I replied.

"Put pressure on it, put pressure on it!" my father retorted contemptuously, as if I had said something completely ridiculous. He didn't know first aid and could not fathom the idea that I might know something he didn't. I experienced many such instances of my father's put-downs, and saw how he ridiculed and belittled my mother. The word patriarchal wasn't in my vocabulary, but I just knew I didn't like his view of me.

My second cousin Ernie, a mathematics professor, lent me his *Complete Sherlock Holmes*, and I spent the rest of that summer reading in bed, cocooned in the spell of the stories, falling in love with the process of unraveling a mystery and discovering the hidden truth. When we left the hotel at the end of the summer, we pushed the door with the broken pane back into the wall, and weren't found out.

Is This Love or Diabetes?

After four years in Oregon, we moved. My father, dissatisfied with his job in Portland, had succumbed to a Boston relative's predictions of a fortune to be made in the cultured pearl business and agreed to start a branch of said relative's company in Chicago. I was devastated. I didn't want to leave Portland. "But you don't have any friends here," said my mother, "so it won't make any difference to you."

How wrong she was! Although my debilitating shyness had prevented me from making friends, I loved our home. I loved Portland, with Mt. Hood always in the background and the pretty flowering trees in spring. I loved our modern ranch house with the huge back yard, and I loved babysitting for little Mikey next door. Even though I couldn't claim any as friends, I admired my classmates at Cedar Hills Junior High, and had looked forward to starting high school with them in the fall.

But I couldn't stop our leaving. My father took us to LA again for the summer, and this time, as a consolation, we got to stay at a motel with a swimming pool. I only ventured away from the place once, to go to a movie, *The Parent Trap*. I was absorbed in the film and barely noticed when a man sat down next to me. Gradually I became aware of a hand slowly moving up my thigh. I got up and switched to a faraway seat, wanting to see the rest of the movie, but after that experience I just stayed around the pool. At the end of the summer, leaving my brother to start Caltech, my parents and I drove to Chicago.

There was nothing pretty about Chicago, and I missed Mt. Hood. I started South Shore High School. The kids my age looked tougher than the Portland kids, and seemed even more sophisticated. There was a two-tiered caste system consisting of the popular kids and the creeps. I was definitely in the latter category. I was miserable. My parents signed me up for Girl

Scouts. My troop consisted of fellow creeps who all loved the activities. I don't remember what these activities were, just that they involved reciting pledges and oaths and getting various badges. To me the whole business was boring and pointless. The one exception was when we learned the Philippine Bamboo Dance for the Girl Scout Jamboree. I really liked learning the tricky steps and performing on stage. We were even on TV. After the jamboree was over, and we were back to the old dull routine, I quit the Girl Scouts.

South Shore High School was housed in an old three-story building. In my sophomore year, I took biology, which was up on the third floor. I developed a crush on a boy named Rich in that class. The class I had just before was in the basement, so I had to race up three flights of stairs to get to biology. I could feel my heart beating faster and faster as I climbed up the stairs. By the time I got to the top floor it would be pounding furiously, and I was feeling so weak and breathless that I could barely stumble into my seat across the aisle from Rich. These feelings, the racing heart, the faintness, this must be love, I thought.

I tried to summon up my courage to let Rich know I liked him. This took a lot of determination, but I managed to start talking to him, and over some weeks I think he got the message that I liked him.

He asked me if I would go out with him. I said yes, but later realized he had been joking. Embarrassed, I pretended I had been joking too. I realized I had been going about it all wrong. If you liked someone, you were supposed to pretend not to like him. There was a girl that he seemed to like who was pretending not to like him, and succeeding in attracting him even more. I felt completely hopeless in this business and often took refuge in a stall of the girls' bathroom to cry.

My mother had noticed that I was drinking a lot of juice at dinner and that I seemed tired. She took me to a doctor, who had instructed her to bring a sample of my urine. He took the jar into another room, and came back in a minute.

"What did you have to eat or drink?" he asked. I said I had drunk four glasses of orange juice. "You've got to get to a hospital right away," he said. "Your urine is full of sugar. Maybe it's just all that orange juice, but I think you have diabetes."

My mother took me to the hospital, and I stayed there for several days while they confirmed that I had diabetes and started giving me insulin shots and a diabetic diet. I became terribly despondent, realizing that this eliminated any chance that I could ever have the life that I secretly dreamed of having one day, the life I saw other kids having, of hanging out with friends and going out on dates and having a boyfriend. How could I be like the other kids if I couldn't eat what they ate? Even if I didn't have this life now, at least I had had hope. Now all hope was gone. I had to count all my food exchanges and from now on french fries and sodas and everything else normal kids ate was out, with artificially sweetened jello called Dzerta taking its place. I was completely miserable, and cried as I practiced giving shots to an orange.

Then a miracle happened. One morning, instead of a shot, I was given two pills. During the day, there were the usual blood and urine tests, but there was no more talk of giving myself shots. The next day I was discharged with a bottle of pills, a roll of special tape to test my urine at home, and a booklet about my diet. It was only much later that I learned the pills were for adult onset diabetes and were not supposed to work for someone my age. A doctor at the hospital whom I never met, whose name I never knew, had thought to try them on me, not expecting them to work. To everyone's complete astonishment, they did work. The pills brought my blood sugar levels back to normal.

After some months, I realized that I didn't have to keep such a strictly regimented diet as the literature and doctors said I did to keep my urine sugar-free. The pills were very forgiving. While I stopped eating candy, cookies, sodas, and cut down on fats, I could eat most things, and grew adept at eliminating starches that I didn't care for anyway. Life was livable again.

One day I got a call from a girl I didn't know, inviting me to join a sorority. I was surprised. I didn't know the girls, and didn't understand why they would want me, but I started pledging. The pledges had to do silly things, like wear odd clothes or a certain number of rollers in our hair, and one time I had to write an essay on the sex life of a marshmallow. I found I liked the girls and that this sorority thing was fun. I was just starting to enjoy myself when my parents announced that we were moving to New York.

A Day to Remember

Most people over a certain age can remember the day John F. Kennedy was shot, and what they were doing then. I can remember that day too, as well as many details of where I was and what I was doing: of the physics class at Forest Hills High School, in Queens, NY, where I first heard of the rumor from a boy behind me; the gym class where the announcement was made and, after a moment of silence, we were told to put our street clothes back on and go home, for school was dismissed. I remember a black girl crying hysterically in the locker room about the war she was sure would come, and me trying uselessly to reassure her. I remember running breathlessly outside to catch up with my friend Jannette.

But all those things were not foremost in my mind. The assassination of JFK took second place for me, for that day was the day of my first date. The day before, a boy had actually asked me out for that evening. Not only that, but it was the boy I had a crush on. His name was Dennis, and he had a headful of beautiful blond curls, twinkling blue eyes, and a cute turned up nose. I couldn't believe it. Maybe now my luck would start to change, and I could be happy. I was worried that maybe the assassination would cancel everything. Maybe my parents would make me stay home, or maybe he wouldn't come. But my parents let me go and he did show up. As soon as we were out of the house I forgot all about the day's events. We went to a bowling alley. I don't remember actually bowling, but I remember a TV set there tuned to the news, bringing the assassination back to me, as well as the proprietor's face, turning in surprise to see us having a good time on such a day.

The Dating Game

During the couple of months I went out with Dennis, I discovered that I had the wonderful power to make a guy desire me. I still had a crush on Dennis and found making out with him intoxicating. It was sexy and exciting and made me feel glamorous, like a movie star. Only Dennis was Catholic, and apparently had been indoctrinated with guilt about sex, for after every passionate clinch he would always apologize with an "I'm sorry."

"For what?" I would ask. I couldn't understand why everyone, even he, thought that what we were doing was bad.

"Does he ever try to kiss you?" my mother asked one time.

"Oh no," I lied, sensing that there was no room for the truth in my parents' mind. Even my one friend, Jannette, disapproved. "You make out with him, don't you?" she accused me contemptuously when I told her I was going to meet Dennis after school. I denied it. Even though I saw nothing wrong with smooching, I wasn't one to assert myself and rock the boat.

Jannette was Chinese-American, and also a social failure, but this was just about the only thing we had in common. She had all the values of our parents' generation, and none of mine. She didn't like rock and roll, distrusted black people, declared she would never stoop to "making out" with a guy, and when her fifteen-year-old younger sister became pregnant and came to her for help, she gave her no sympathy, only a lecture about her shameful condition. Still, she was the only friend I had, and as outcasts desperate for companionship, we stuck together. We'd chat on the phone, went clothes shopping together in Manhattan, and walked home with each other after school.

By that time, my mother had become extremely critical of me, and my father always backed her negative views of me.

According to them, I was selfish, self-centered, and only cared about myself. There was no real reason for their complaints, for I was always obedient at home and school, did my chores, got straight A's, made my pocket money babysitting, and never got into any trouble. Looking back on it, I think that seeing me having what appeared on the surface to be a carefree adolescence may have reminded my mother of what had been denied her, and this may have caused her to resent me. One time I entered the living room unnoticed by my mother, who was talking on the phone to a friend or relative. She was complaining about me, saying how one of her children, my brother, had turned out so good, while the other was "a bad seed." I felt like I'd been stabbed, and quietly left the room without being noticed.

After a couple of months Dennis quit school and, lying about his age, joined the Navy. I soon had other boys asking me out, and went through a rapid succession of short-term boyfriends. I don't think I ever had a conversation with any of them. I had no idea how to talk to anyone, but I excelled in the art of making out. It felt so good to be wanted. However, I had no intention of going all the way and risking getting pregnant.

"Has a boy ever tried to touch you there?" asked my mother.

"Oh no," I said, for I had been taught to comply with what was expected of me, and so kept quiet, and made sure to always get home by the time my parents told me to.

One time I came home from school to find my parents seething with indignation at me. This was nothing new, for they always seemed to find something wrong with me.

"What is it this time?" I wondered.

"You didn't lock the outer door when you went out this morning," they said. "and something very bad happened." We lived in a duplex. Someone had knocked at the door of the other apartment, and the elderly woman who lived there had opened it, expecting it to be one of us, for the front doorbell had not rung. Instead, she saw a *black* man, and almost died of fright. It turned out he was a utility company employee, there to read the meter, but to my parents my thoughtlessness had caused the near-death of our neighbor. I was a self-absorbed girl who didn't care about other people. The fact that the man had done no harm paled in comparison to what, in their minds, he was *likely* to have done.

I felt more and more that I had to get away from my parents.

The summer before my senior year in high school, my mother's cousin Ilse invited me to spend a couple of weeks in Boston with her family. She had a daughter, my second cousin Jona, who was a year older than I. Jona was an outgoing girl with lots of friends, and I was accepted into her group without question. Suddenly I was leading the life of a normal teenager. We'd hang out at the beach, go to movies, listen to music together. Although I was still too inhibited to speak, I was having fun, something that was absent from my life at home. My cousin's home life with her family seemed so pleasant too, so relaxed and accepting. Jona introduced me to Gary, who was a student at Boston University, and I went out with him to folk music cafes. I remember we saw Jim Kweskin's Jug Band. I was also introduced to the records of folk singers such as Joan Baez. I extended my visit in Boston as long as I could. It was really hard going back to my life back home. I decided that I just had to go away to college. My parents wanted me to go to Queens College and live at home. The fact that I wanted to leave them was, to my parents, another sign of my selfishness.

I thought of becoming a nurse. Inspired by TV doctor shows like Ben Casey and Dr. Kildare, I thought a medical career would be exciting. I had applied to the Bachelor of Science in Nursing program at Hunter College, which required students to reside at the school. I expected to get in, since I had straight A's and very high SAT scores. However, my parents contacted the director and told her that I was a diabetic, and

51

that the demands of nursing would be too strenuous for me. My nursing career was nipped in the bud, but I had other options, having applied to other schools. I was accepted at Sarah Lawrence, but the partial scholarship they offered me was not enough to make this private college affordable. My third choice was SUNY at Stony Brook, and I was ecstatic on the day the letter came telling me that I had received a full Regents scholarship. Now there was nothing to stop me from leaving in the fall.

Yet there was still the rest of the school year and the long summer. My father, tired of working for others, had decided to go into business for himself. Wanting to buy a franchise, he considered two options, Chicken Delight or Dairy Queen. He chose the latter.

Dairy Queen

It all started out a happy and exciting day. It was our last day of preparation, for tomorrow was the grand opening. We did all the innumerable things that had to be done: packing the different flavors, mixing in fruits and nuts, making all the ice cream products, arranging posters on the walls, and cleaning, cleaning, and more cleaning. There was so much to be done, but we did it all, my mother, father, and myself. Finally we were finished. I was exhausted, but happy, for I loved fixing things up, making something look beautiful. I put away the mop and took a Dilly Bar, one of the round Dairy Queen ice cream popsicles. I had made them that morning, dispensing dozens of disks of soft ice cream and inserting a stick into each, then letting them freeze hard. Later I dipped each one in a chocolate coating and wrapped the finished products. Now I peeled off the paper from one and bit through its chocolatey coating into the creamy center.

I was jarred out of my enjoyment by my mother's screams. "Look at her, eating ice cream! Here we are, working ourselves to death, and it's all just going to be wasted on her medical bills."

I put away the ice cream bar. I couldn't taste it any longer, couldn't swallow. Her words hurt more than if she'd hit me. What was worse, they were untrue. Sure, I had diabetes. I'd been diagnosed less than two years ago, when I was fifteen. But my mother knew it was under control. I hadn't had any problems with it, and the large medical bills she was blaming me for were nonexistent, a product of her tendency to blame me for everything that frightened her.

Well, the Dairy Queen opened the next day. I worked there every day after school, and on weekends and holidays. My mother never saw me eat ice cream again, although it made up a large percentage of my diet at the Dairy Queen, together with all the toppings I could pile up on it and consume in the back of the store. I became very good at eating stealthily. Funny, all that ice cream didn't seem to affect my health, thanks to the pills I was taking and avoidance of other starches. My doctor, whom I saw about twice a year for a blood sugar test, which was always perfect, always commended me on my ability to stick to a diabetic diet. Little did he know that I only ate carefully on the few days before the test!

However, I became more and more unhappy working for my father at the Dairy Queen, and was also miserable at home with my parents. Every moment spent in their company was a reminder of what a bad person I was. Their beloved business was all they talked about, and not understanding why I wasn't as smitten with the family endeavor as they were, they branded me a selfish, uncaring girl. I tried to get away as much as I could when I wasn't working. Since I was too shy to be outgoing, this was a difficulty.

I needed a boyfriend who could take me away from my parents in my free time. One soon appeared. His name was Ira, and he worked at the pharmacy across the street from the Dairy Queen. Soon after we opened, I noticed him coming in regularly. He was tall and not bad looking, so when he asked me out to a movie, I accepted. I don't remember the movie, but I remember that afterwards, he expected more than just the making out I knew. He demanded satisfaction. This was going further than I was comfortable with, but I complied because he seemed my only chance for brief respites from my parents. I went out with him all of that summer. Although he was obsessed with sex, he didn't insist on going all the way because I was, as he termed it, "jailbait." He said he would wait until I turned 18, making do with everything else till then. I was glad that my 18th birthday was not until October, when I would be at college, far away from him, my parents, and the Dairy Queen.

Fall finally arrived, and I started school at Stony Brook. My roommate Ethel, an outgoing black girl from Brooklyn, was soon the hub of a busy social circle. I tried to make friends with her, but was too inept socially. I soon found that I was being left out of her crowd, and became very lonely. I hooked up with the first guy who asked me, and was relieved that this thing called virginity that everyone seemed so hung up about disappeared promptly on my 18th birthday. The guy was annoyingly insecure and was upset that I was getting A's on my exams, while he was failing. I was relieved when he flunked out at the end of the semester and left. Now I appreciated being alone and free again. I got a work-study job in the school cafeteria, and between that and studies, the school year passed.

It was time to go back to my parents and work at the Dairy Queen for the summer. Nine months had passed. Maybe it wouldn't be so bad, I thought, but the very first day at DQ I realized it was even worse than I remembered. My mother criticized me more than ever. She seemed jealous of the independence I'd had in school. My father acted hurt that I didn't seem to care as much about the business as he did. They both constantly let me know that I was a self-centered girl who didn't care about her family. I didn't see how I could stand the summer there.

You may wonder why I didn't just go apply for a job elsewhere. First, there was the fact that it would not have been possible to live with my parents if I did, for they didn't comprehend my need for independence, would have seen my actions as treason, and I could not afford to pay for my own place. Also, in the mid-sixties, a young woman in New York on her own was a target. There were many times I'd been groped or propositioned, or both, just walking down the street in broad daylight. I'd also been groped in the subway when Jannette and I were on our shopping trips to Manhattan.

Ira still worked at the pharmacy, and asked me out again that first day back. I realized what that meant, now that I wasn't jailbait anymore. I weighed my options. I desperately needed some escape from my parents' critical eyes 24 hours a day, seven days a week. I didn't know anyone else who would ask me out. He wasn't bad looking, and I liked sex, if not his personality. He was so narrow-minded, but I thought I could put up with him for the summer. So I went out with him. By juggling Ira and the Dairy Queen and my parents, I managed to survive the summer, but just barely. As soon as it was time to go back to school, I broke up with Ira and vowed to myself that I would never submit to this miserable life again, would never again live in my parents' home, never work at the Dairy Queen again, and never again have sex with someone I didn't like.

The first semester of my sophomore year turned out uneventful. Again I did well in school and made dean's list, worked in the cafeteria, and wished I had friends but was too shy to do anything about it. I had a new roommate, for Ethel had decided to room with one of her friends and I asked another loner to room with me. We had nothing in common except for our social isolation, for she was very religious and only tolerated classical music. I developed a crush on this guy, Seth, but he didn't seem interested in me. He was also from Forest Hills, however, and gave me a ride home for the Christmas break. I couldn't think of a single thing to say to him on the way home.

The Dairy Queen, fortunately, was closed during the winter break, so I didn't have to work there. Ira, however, was there waiting for me. He wanted to take me out for New Year's Eve, he said; just as a friend, he said; he wouldn't touch me, he promised. He was very proud of having joined an exclusive fraternity, the first Jew ever to be accepted, and they were having this really fantastic party and he was sure I'd have a really great time. To my surprise my mother also urged me to go with him. Apparently he had continued coming into the Dairy Queen and had been working his charm on my mother, giving her a sob story of how I'd broken his heart.

Anyway, I accepted, and went out with him as "just friends" to the party. It was in some secluded cabin in the woods, miles away from anything. I had gone shopping with Jannette just days before and bought this cute silver-striped mini-dress at Macy's. I felt good in my new outfit, but as soon as I walked into the large room, I saw another girl wearing an identical one. She gave me a freezing look. I got the cold shoulder from everyone else too. I realized these were all fraternity and sorority guys and girls who all knew each other, and they were not kind to outsiders. I started drinking, but that didn't ease my discomfort. Finally, I couldn't stand it any longer.

"I'd like to go home now," I said to Ira.

"I'll only take you home if you agree to have sex with me," he said in a loud voice, loud enough for everyone to hear.

Suddenly, I was the center of everyone's undivided attention, and they seemed very interested in what I had to say. I was tipsy enough to oblige them.

"Take me home right now, you disgusting jerk," I screamed, "and I wouldn't touch you with a ten-foot pole."

We drove off. However, there were miles of deserted woods between me and home. I knew he wouldn't let me go so easily. I wasn't consciously thinking of a plan. I was too drunk, but when he stopped and parked the car in some desolate spot, something inside me knew exactly what to do.

I started crying. Not just a few tears, but desperate wails and loud moans and cries to wake the dead. This wasn't hard to do, in my drunken state. All I had to do was summon up an image in my mind of Seth, my secret crush, and how he didn't love me, and out would come a heartbroken shriek of grief, and then I'd think of how he would never love me, and I would be overcome with incredible racking sobs of despair. Ira was completely confused by this and didn't know what to make of it. "Naomi, stop crying," he kept pleading, but I didn't stop. At that point, I couldn't stop. My crying had started as a lifeline, but now it had a life of its own. Eventually he gave up, started the engine, and drove me home. As soon as we got there I jumped out of the car, my tears magically drying up, and ran to the door. I never saw him again, I'm glad to say. My mother told me that for a long time afterwards he would complain to her of how cruelly and heartlessly I had treated him. She thought he was the ideal Jewish boy for me, and that I was hardhearted for rejecting him. I wondered what she'd think of him if she knew what he was really like.

Changing

Breaking Free

A short while after the spring semester started, I got a letter from Boston, from my old friend Gary. I didn't consider Gary to be my boyfriend, but I liked him. I had written him about my unhappiness at home. In his letter back he invited me to stay with him over the spring break, for he had his own apartment in Brookline, near Boston. I definitely wanted to accept, but what about my parents? They would be really upset about me staying in a guy's apartment. He came up with a great idea. I would tell my parents that I was staying with Margie, a friend of his who was willing to help, and give my parents her address and phone number. If they called there, she would say that I was out, call me at Gary's place, and then I could call them back saying I just got in. So that's what I did, and the two weeks I spent with Gary were blissful. We became lovers, and Gary suggested I come back to live with him over the summer. I accepted, but knew that there was no way I could keep up the pretense for three months. I would have to tell my parents that I was living with Gary. I thought it best to wait until I was settled in before breaking the news to them, so I told them I was going back to stay with Margie again for the first week of summer before coming home. When I got to Brookline, I found a job waitressing at a downtown Boston cafe. The week went by, then two weeks, and my parents were getting impatient for me to come home. There was no way I could delay the inevitable any more, and I finally wrote them that I was staying with Gary for the summer, that I was happy with him and that I wasn't happy living at home and working at the Dairy Queen, that I had a job in Boston and would go back to Stony Brook in the fall.

I had expected them to be very upset, and they were. I

wasn't surprised when my mother said I was no longer her daughter. What surprised me, however, was that they were just as upset by the fact that I didn't want to work at the DQ as the fact that I was living with a man. To them this rejection of the family business was the ultimate betrayal, and my father was terribly hurt. He said I would regret this and that I would get no more money from them. I reminded them that I was self-sufficient and had been for some time, for I had a full scholarship, a summer job, and a job at school as well. However, for my parents this was an issue of me shirking my duty.

The summer was life-changing for me. I was not only free of my parents, but suddenly my social status skyrocketed. I went from being a social outcast to being one of the "in crowd," for I was the girlfriend of the lead singer of a popular local rock band. Gary's band played at a lot of places in Boston. Though I still felt the same crippling awkwardness inside, I basked in Gary's reflected glory.

We went to see many of the big groups, like Cream, when they came to Boston. I had always loved rock music, but previously I only listened secretly, alone in my room. Now I grew to love being surrounded by it. I have a happy memory of Gary's clock radio waking us one morning with a new Beatles song, "All You Need is Love." Gary introduced me to marijuana, but it didn't seem to affect me at all, and I didn't see what the fuss was about. At first I enjoyed playing house with Gary, but after a while I noticed that he sometimes had dark moods, when he could be quite nasty. When fall came, he wanted me to stay there with him, but I decided to go back to school.

I started my junior year at Stony Brook. Now I was back to being an outsider, and terribly lonely again. Gary said he missed me too, and wrote that he needed me, wanted to marry me, that I should quit school and live with him for good. I didn't know what to do. In desperation I called Hanan, who was in grad school at Columbia studying nuclear physics. I had visited there once, bringing him a Bob Dylan album, but I got the feeling my musical offering was viewed with the same condescending eye with which my parents saw all of my endeavors. He was pursuing a narrow academic path. I felt that we had nothing in common. Still, he was my brother. I asked if I could come see him, that I needed to talk to him, but he said that there was nothing he could do to help me. "I get depressed sometimes too, thinking what it's all for," he said, "and then I just sit and watch the fish in my aquarium."

It was one of the worst days I'd ever had. I had to make a terribly important decision, to marry or stay in school, and I just didn't know what to do, or where to turn. I took a shower and washed my hair. When I finished, my mind was made up. I was going to stay in school.

I still went back to visit Gary sometimes, catching a cheap commuter flight from New York to Boston for a couple of days at a time. He was becoming more and more demanding, phoning and getting mad if I wouldn't fly out to see him right away.

A Chance Encounter

One day I was on the Long Island Railroad making my way back to school. As the train crawled along the countless stations spread across the length of Long Island, rattling from one creaky groaning stop to the next, I was content to sink into my usual daydreaming haze. Finally, the train arrived at the Stony Brook station. Stumbling out, I noticed a tall young man heading towards the campus, which was about a mile away. Stony Brook was a brand new school, with unfinished buildings all around. There was no path connecting the campus with the train station yet. One just had to maneuver one's way around the numerous construction sites. The day was warm and the snow in the fields was melting into a brown slush. I was still in an unfocused state from the train ride and started following the guy without thinking. After we had been wading through the muck for some time, I noticed that we had somehow wound up in the middle of a construction site which was obviously the wrong place.

"Say, do you know the way to the dorms?" he asked me.

"No," I said, "I was following you. I thought you knew the way."

His name was Steve, he said, and he was coming back from his parents' home in Brooklyn. He had black curly hair and glasses. We eventually managed to find our way to campus, and went to our separate dorms.

A few days later, when I was working behind the counter in the cafeteria during lunch, putting chocolate puddings on the counter, I noticed him going by in line. He started mumbling something at me, but I couldn't understand what he was saying. "What? What did you say?" I called after him, for he was quickly moving on past me.

"Umm, the poet, the poet."

I had no idea what he was talking about, and he

disappeared. When I finished work, I discovered Steve lurking behind a pillar just outside the cafeteria, puffing on a harmonica. "I meant Allen Ginsberg," he said, "I just couldn't think of his name. You know he's speaking in the gym tonight. Wanna go see him?"

"OK," I said happily.

I remember nothing about Allen Ginsberg or the poetry reading, but I remember going to the woods after the show with Steve and a bunch of his friends and smoking hash with them. Then Steve and I went to his dorm room. He took out a guitar.

"What's your favorite song?" he asked.

As usual, my mind went blank.

"I can play any song," he boasted. "Do you like the Beatles?"

"Yes," I said. He proceeded to sing and play each and every Beatles song, going through dozens of them. He really did know them all, and he played them sublimely, not just strumming the chords but plucking the strings deftly in a way I'd never seen before.

"How did you learn to play like that?" I asked.

"My parents made me take violin lessons since I was little, and when I started liking the guitar, it was easy to pick it up from records. I listen to a lot of blues records and play along. Those old guys, Leadbelly and Robert Johnson, they're the best." He went on to play "Goodnight, Irene" and other blues numbers.

He serenaded me all night as I watched his long slender fingers caress the strings, so delicately yet so surely. I longed to reach over, take the guitar out of his hands, and slide into its place, but as usual was too timid to make a move. By the time morning came, I was in love with Steve.

Little did I know what I was in for.

Changes

Then came our second date. I didn't really care where we went or what we did. I was too much in awe of him. He was one of the popular guys, always with a crowd of friends around him, with usually at least one girl hanging on his arm or sitting on his lap in the cafeteria. I, with no friends and much too shy, ate my meals alone. I was not in a position to ask questions.

We were going to the campus bookstore. Everyone hated it. They grossly overcharged us, but there was no place else, stuck as we were in the middle of the woods in the middle of Long Island, to get our textbooks and the other things we needed.

We went over to the records section. He told me to go over to the saleswoman and ask her to help me find something. I did just that. I knew what he was doing in the meantime. I didn't care. I felt no loyalty to the bookstore or anyone else.

After we were outside and around the corner he took them out. Steve was big, 6'3", and they had all fit nicely under his leather jacket, about six of the latest albums: The Doors, Bob Dylan, Jefferson Airplane, Rolling Stones, etc.

We walked back to his dorm room. His friends were there. He started handing out the records, giving them all away, laughing and boasting about how he had stolen them. It was then that I started feeling nauseous.

He walked me back to my dorm. It was good to be out of his room, back in the cold winter air. I felt some relief, yet still I found strange words suddenly coming out of my mouth. "You're just a big showoff. You stole those records just to buy friends."

To my astonishment, he started crying. "If that's what you think of me, why are you going out with me?"

I was afraid to tell him the truth, afraid to say "I only realized these things just now," afraid it would make him weep again. Instead I mumbled some cliché about how this was only the way he was on the surface, and that I knew he was really a fine person on the inside. This seemed to satisfy him, however, and he smiled shyly at me.

I guess you could say that this incident changed me. I felt that I had discovered something amazing. For the first time I realized that other people could be as vulnerable and scared as I was, in spite of seeming so sure of themselves and being popular. This started me on the long road to becoming less afraid of people. It was something I had to tackle because I wanted to be with Steve, and he was always with people. He was not satisfied to be with just me for very long; he liked to have his buddies around him. I, on the other hand, was very uncomfortable with his friends and could only relax after they were gone and I was alone with Steve.

I decided to try the campus psych services. I got an appointment with a therapist and told him of the anxiety I felt when I was with people. He asked me to think of the moment when I started feeling tense in a social situation.

"Why, I get anxious as soon as I see someone and think I might be expected to talk to them. Even if someone is just approaching to pass by me on one of the paths on campus, I get nervous wondering if and how I should say hi to them."

"OK," he said, "now we know where to start."

He showed me a room specially equipped with a recliner and a tape recorder with headphones. I was to come in every day and lie down and listen to a tape which taught me how to gradually relax each muscle in my body. After a few weeks, when I had learned to relax completely, I went through another tape, this time picturing someone approaching me as I tried to maintain a relaxed state. I spent several months with the tapes, gradually working towards slightly more demanding social situations. Then the therapist told me he was leaving for another job on the west coast, taking his tapes with him. I was sorry to see him go, but I knew that what he had taught me would stay with me. I now knew that my social awkwardness was not something intrinsically wrong with me. I could change. I realized that being with Steve and his entourage, as difficult as it was for me, would help me change.

* * *

When Steve's father bought himself a new car, he gave Steve the old one. Steve was very happy, but not as happy as his friends at Stony Brook, for now they wouldn't have to chauffeur him around anymore. He was constantly on the go, and always persuading someone to pick him up here, give him a ride there, just one more trip into the city, etc.

But actually, now that he had the car, the problems were just starting. First, he was a terrible driver, and second, he was always misplacing his car. He not only forgot where he had parked it, he could not remember what it looked like. Both problems stemmed from his terrible absentmindedness. He'd forget what he was doing, start talking to his friends in the car, forget the road and . . . crash. He got into so many accidents that soon his car was covered with big dents. This was an advantage, however, for it helped him with his second problem, locating his misplaced car. "I just look for a car that's the most smashed looking, and that's mine," he'd say.

Fortunately, he had not been involved in any serious accidents. Still, I was becoming uneasy. I'd always have to remind him to watch the road. One time, he was talking animatedly at me sitting next to him, and I noticed that we were coming to a T intersection, with the road ending ahead as it branched to the left and right at the foot of a grassy hill. Steve's head was turned towards me and I wondered what would happen if I didn't say anything. Well, sure enough, he was so engrossed in what he was saying that he didn't notice.

He just kept going straight off the road, straight up the hill. He didn't notice until we drove into a tree. Fortunately, the steep ascent had cut our speed to a crawl. After that I decided not to ride with him anymore.

Another aspect of his absentmindedness was that he was always losing stuff, leaving his books and things in his various classrooms and the cafeteria. Also, he had a hard time distinguishing between what belonged to him and what belonged to others. If he went to visit a friend, he was more likely than not to leave with his friend's jacket, and leave his own behind. This he did unconsciously, for he really seldom knew what his things looked like.

You may wonder why, with these faults, he had so many loyal friends. Well, he had many endearing qualities also. One was that he wrote his friends' English papers. He loved to string words together, whether orally or in writing. It was a pleasure to watch him write. He had no need of making a rough draft. He just sat at a typewriter, the keys raining down steadily without a break, while sheet after completed sheet drifted to the floor. He had incredibly long fingers, and the fact that he had played violin since he was seven had given them a life of their own. Thus he was a very fast typist. He told how he would walk into secretarial employment agencies looking for a summer job. The receptionist and all those coifed and polished girls would look askance at his long hair and bell bottoms. But then it would be time for the typing test. "I'd leave all those girls far behind, for I can type up a storm, and I'd get the best paying job."

Because he was always losing things like his books, he always had to replenish his supply by stealing from stores, and this he did easily, for his long, quick fingers helped him develop this into an art. He seldom walked out of a store without something he hadn't paid for hidden somewhere on him; sometimes it would be a half dozen books or records stuffed against the back of his jacket, sometimes just a little trinket up his sleeve. He would often be surprised at what he found later in his pockets. He never kept anything he stole. He either gave it away or quickly lost it again.

His most memorable theft happened just after his grandmother died. He had been very close to Nana, for it was she who had raised him. His mother had emotional problems and had been unable to care for him much of the time. I had met Nana. She was very old, and hunchbacked since childhood.

"She always wanted me to massage her hump, since I was little, for it hurt her," he said. "I'm so glad I did that for her." He came back to my dorm from the funeral, red-eyed and holding a enormous bouquet of beautiful flowers. He had gathered them from nearby graves. "Flowers should be for the living," he said, holding them out to me.

Bob's Sheet

Steve lived in the dorm next to mine, with a roommate named Bob. Steve and Bob were good friends, and got along in most ways except one. Bob was very neat and finicky about his clothes and possessions, while Steve was sloppy and careless to an extreme. They resolved this discrepancy by dividing their room straight down the middle. While this was a working compromise, Bob was always somewhat anxious about the chaos that seemed to be forever on the verge of overflowing onto his territory, while Steve had to constantly fight the temptation of trampling onto the pristine purity that beckoned from Bob's side.

One day I came over just as Bob was leaving to go to a chemistry lab class. "Look, Steve," said Bob, "I just put clean sheets on my bed. The bedspread is still in the dryer, so don't sit on my bed, you hear? Just stay off it!"

Steve assured him that he had nothing to worry about, but as soon as the door closed, Steve eyed Bob's snow-white sheets hungrily.

"C'mon, let's do it on his bed," he murmured as he pulled me towards Bob's side of the room.

"But Steve, you know he just told you to leave his bed alone!" I protested.

"It'll be better on his bed," Steve insisted. "I'll be careful. He'll never find out." No matter how I tried to maneuver him onto his own bed, Steve had his heart set, and we wound up on his roommate's virginal sheets. I must say there something to Steve's claim, for sex on Bob's bed really was fantastic. Afterwards, we fell into a deep, satisfied sleep.

I awoke a couple of hours later to the familiar cramps that always signaled the beginning of my period. I checked, and sure enough, there was a bright red stain on the sheet. Immediately realizing the implications, I jumped up, threw on my clothes and shook Steve awake. "Get up," I cried, pointing out the spot. "I'll throw the sheet into the washer so it'll be clean when he gets back."

"No time," said Steve, looking at the clock. "He's due back any minute."

"But Steve, he'll be furious when he sees what we did to his clean sheet."

Realizing that something had to be done, Steve grabbed a thick black wax pencil from Bob's desk, the kind used to mark laboratory glassware, and with a few wide marks covered the bloody part completely so that it was now a big black spot instead. "There," he said, "you can't see it anymore."

I looked incredulously at what he had done. "Now it's worse," I screamed at him. "You've made it even more noticeable and impossible to wash out." Noting the logic of my words, Steve decided to end the problem once and for all. A pair of scissors suddenly appeared in his hand and before I could stop him, he had cut out the black spot.

I stared aghast at the hole. "You've completely ruined his sheet. He'll kill you."

Again Steve had to concede that I was right. But he didn't panic. Instead he went over to his own bed and cut a hole in his sheet, the same size as the one in Bob's sheet. He put the scissors away and had just finished putting on his clothes when Bob walked in the door.

"Look at that!" announced Steve indignantly. "Some joker cut holes in our sheets while we were out. I bet it's that smart-aleck Harvey next door. He's always playing these stupid practical jokes."

Bob was so upset and angry at Harvey that he didn't notice my inadequate attempts at a straight face and the stifled choking sounds escaping as I hurriedly left the room.

Manhattan

Now, you may be thinking, what about Gary, in Boston? Well, I'd written him a letter saying that I didn't think we were right for each other. I also told him I was seeing someone else. I didn't hear back from him and thought that was the end of it.

One day, at the end of the school year just before finals, I came back from class to my dorm room, opened the door, and there he was, standing there, waiting for me, hands behind his back.

"Come in and close the door," he said. Foolishly, I obeyed, too stunned to do anything else.

"Lie down on the bed," he continued. I was frozen, unable to move, but then I caught a flash of a blade in his hand. That did it, the spell was broken, and I screamed the loudest scream anyone has ever screamed, a scream so loud I was sure that everyone in the entire building would come rushing to my rescue immediately. Now it was Gary's turn to be stunned. He stared at me dumbfounded for a second, then mumbling, "Man, you sure can yell," and "I was only going to cut your hair," ran out of my room and disappeared, taking what I now saw was a large pair of scissors with him.

I stood shaking in my room for a little while, waiting for everyone to come to find out why I screamed. After a while I tentatively opened the door and peeked out. There was nobody there. I looked further. The whole dorm was deserted. Everyone must have been in class or studying for finals somewhere else. I went back in my room, and that's when I discovered that Gary had ransacked my desk and taken all of my class notes, which I needed for my finals. I was upset, but managed to do fine on my finals anyway, and was kind of glad that I had that much less to study.

This was the end of my junior year. Steve and I decided we'd get an apartment and work in Manhattan for the summer. He found a place for us, on the Upper West Side, for $90 a month. The kitchen was full of cockroaches. We could hear them rustling around at night. Our bed was next to the window, and the sheets used to get covered with soot. Still, I was happy living there with Steve. I found a job working in a jewelry factory but quit after a couple of weeks because of the sleazy boss. He used to call me into his office, telling me of his love for Israel and of his son who had just had his Bar Mitzvah, but soon the talk would change to how he'd love to spank me. Fortunately, a friend of Steve's who was working for a stock market publisher told Steve they needed more people, and we both wound up getting hired there.

I liked this job. It involved using a rapidograph to draw the stock charts for the publications. This was as close as I had come to an artistic career, and it fitted my leaning towards careful, precise work. It also paid very well, and we realized we'd even have enough money to take a two-week camping vacation in the national park on St. John's Island in the Caribbean before school started in the fall. I drew the charts for the weekly publication, and always took care that my graphs were accurate and flawless. Steve worked on the graphs that only came out every three months, and realizing that his work would not be published until a few days after we left, he just drew them whichever way he felt like. He jokingly wondered how many Wall Street investors would jump out of windows due to his faulty charts.

CL

She was my roommate in our senior year at Stony Brook. Steve had suggested we room together. She was one of his many friends, or had been, for lately she seemed to harbor some kind of resentment toward him. "I'm not playing your games any more, Steven," she suddenly announced one day as several of us were walking together, and never talked to him again after that. She gave no explanation.

"Schizophrenic," said Steve dismissively. There were quite a few people she wouldn't talk to, for no reason I could discern.

CL were not her initials. Her name was Leslie Ross. CL stood for Crazy Leslie. Howie gave her that name. Howie gave everyone their nicknames, including his own, "the Pig." These names, though often unflattering, didn't seem to offend the bearers, for we seemed to recognize the fit, and accepted them, and they stuck throughout the years. I was "Robin Block Bizarro," shortened to Bizarro, due to my resemblance to another girl. I felt rather flattered, for I considered Robin Block quite pretty. Being a weird version of beautiful Robin seemed better than being my ordinary self. Leslie also did not seem to mind her nickname.

She seemed to like me, or at least didn't mind me, though I didn't know the reason for that either. We really didn't seem to have anything in common, and rarely talked. I guess I was a little afraid of her. Her appearance itself was unsettling. She had a pale, white, gaunt face with stark cheekbones, huge blue-black slightly bulging eyes topped with thick mascara, a slender hawklike nose, and masses of black hair which she spent hours fixing in front of the mirror, finally emerging with it looking exactly as when she had started: a scrambled, mangled nest of thorns. She looked somewhere between regal and witchlike, and definitely intimidating.

Yet there was a wild kind of vulnerability in her eyes sometimes, a helplessness that was disturbing. You felt that she might break, not, as Bob Dylan would have it, like a little girl, but like glass, into sharp jagged pieces that could tear and cut. Her mouth would occasionally, unexpectedly, break into a big, wide smile.

She was incredibly sloppy. This was a boon to me, for I was relieved to finally find someone messier than I was. However, it became hard to maneuver around our room, for the floor was covered with junk. Once, on a whim, I decided to clean up. I took whatever I found on the floor, hair rollers, wads of tissues with makeup on them, etc., and tacked them to the wall. They looked pretty nice up there. From then on, that's how we kept our room clean.

We shared a dorm suite with Ellen, aka the Lizardess, who dyed all her clothes, sheets, and curtains purple, and Jill, whose wardrobe consisted solely of black leotards.

When we first roomed together, CL's boyfriend was Brian, nicknamed "the Junkie." One night she came in very stoned and screaming hysterically that he had been telling her that her skin was crawling with bugs. Shortly afterwards, he was busted and sentenced to three months in jail. She refused to visit him in prison. Instead, she started going out with a guy known as "the Freak," whom I had noticed because of his amazing drawings of skeletons in various poses. He was into doing threesomes with CL and her best friend Mary Beth, over in G dorm. Leslie was in love with him, and as crazy and wild as she appeared to be, what was happening greatly distressed her.

It was then that Little Andy wrote her the letter. He was known as Little Andy, though he was well over six feet tall, because he was only sixteen and the youngest student at our university. He brought out all of our maternal instincts, and because of a housing shortage in the dorms, had been camping on a mattress in our living room since the beginning of the school year. CL and Little Andy had become close friends and confidants, and he was also friends with the Freak. Little Andy had tried to talk sense to CL about her infatuation. He knew everything about the Freak, and told her that the Freak didn't really care about her and was just using her sexually. But CL was beyond the point of listening to reason.

Then Little Andy wrote CL the letter. She showed it to me, dumbfounded and at a complete loss as to what to do about it. For in that letter Little Andy confessed that he was in love with her. He could no longer hide his feelings under the guise of friendship.

It was just after this letter that the notorious incident took place in G dorm. CL had been over there as usual with the Freak and Mary Beth, but this time she came back in a state of complete shock.

"He pissed out the window," she said, horrified. "He didn't feel like walking to the toilet, so he just opened the window, and . . ." the pain in her eyes stopped her. It was the final indignity.

It was then that the change in CL took place. The change that no one expected, which none of us would have guessed could happen to her. It was because of Peter, a red-haired kid nobody had noticed before. He started calling her, and she became different, almost overnight it seemed. Her eyes now had a shiny, glazed look. She talked differently too. Peter and Leslie would sit in the living room chanting, "Nam Yoho Renge Kyo, Nam Yoho Renge Kyo," for hours to each other, driving a crazed Little Andy to look for other living arrangements. Peter and Leslie's eyes started looking the same and they started sounding the same, saying you could get anything you wanted just by chanting for it. Leslie was smiling all the time now, but I felt like she had died.

Berkeley 1969

June 3, 1969, was my graduation day. I had made it through four years of college at Stony Brook as an honor student. Unlike some of my classmates, I hadn't fallen under the spell of either cults or drugs. I avoided anything that promised spiritual rewards because I could smell phoniness a mile away, and although I had tried many drugs, the only ones that really appealed to me were the psychedelics, with their marvelous visual effects. However, they made me feel awful physically, so that while some of my classmates had tripped several times a week, I braved my nausea only once or twice a year.

I now had my bachelor's degree, but I didn't attend my graduation. I was on a San Francisco-bound plane that day. San Francisco, I had heard, was a wonderful place. I had with me a very small suitcase, what was left of my earnings from working in the school cafeteria, and a slip of paper with the name and number of a friend of a friend of Steve, who, having failed his horseback riding class, had to stay another semester in college to complete his physical education requirement.

I fought off an insignificant panic as I realized that I had no definite idea of where I would stay that night. But it was going to be great there. I was leaving dismal gray New York for a beautiful paradise. Everything would be fine.

I told myself that I could always stay at a hotel, but I knew I couldn't afford anything expensive, and from what I knew of Manhattan's seedy hotels, the thought of a cheap hotel in a strange city was not comforting. But I fought the panic and focused on the elation. It was going to be great there. San Francisco was a beautiful place. And I was free. For the first time in my life, I was completely and absolutely free: free of school, free of my parents. It was going to be great.

I called the number from the San Francisco airport. Luck

was with me. He was home and yes, I could stay at his place for a few days. What a relief! He told me which bus to take. I was pleasantly surprised by the hilly terrain and the colorful buildings. Like in a storybook, I thought, such pretty houses, so many hills.

When I got off the bus I realized that the address was on the top of the steepest hill I could ever have imagined. I trudged on up, lugging my suitcase, which had strangely grown to an enormous size and weight. But I reached the house and met my host. He pointed out the mattress I could sleep on in the spare room, told me to help myself in the kitchen, showed me where the extra key was hidden outside, recommended that I visit Berkeley, and promptly bid me goodbye, as he was going out for the evening. I never saw him again.

When I found myself alone in the house, the day's stress and the enormity of my situation began to sink in. I was completely alone and 3,000 miles away from everything familiar. But even as I cried myself to sleep, I realized that I was somehow very, very happy.

The next day I took the bus for Berkeley. That day is an enchanted blur in my memory. Lovely images delighting my senses: the ride across the Bay Bridge over the sparkling water; walking down the streets with the hills on one side and the bay on the other; friendly people who smiled at me on the sidewalk and didn't hassle me. Definitely very unlike New York. Sitting on the grassy slopes of the UC Berkeley campus, I felt that I wanted to stay here forever, to live here, to make this my home.

I don't remember how I found it. It was listed on some bulletin board, I think, but I found a room for rent. Some newlywed couple was renting out a room in their apartment in order to stretch their budget. I took it, went back to the apartment in San Francisco and got my suitcase, left a thank you note for my host, and moved to Berkeley.

The room at the newlyweds' turned out to be not that great. Although they were both nice and friendly towards me, I got the impression that they would rather be alone with each other. So I looked around for something else.

At the same time, I looked for a job on campus. I inquired in the zoology department office for openings and was sent up to the fifth floor. At the end of a dark and gloomy hall reeking of a strange musty combination of chemical and animal smells, I found an ancient-looking laboratory and a white-haired professor. He needed an assistant for his research with fruit flies, he said in a thick German accent. I told him I had just gotten a BS in biological sciences.

"Can you, by any chance, read German?" he inquired.

I assured him that I could read as well as speak German. The job, which was for ten months, would not start for another three weeks, and there were some other applicants to consider, he said, but he promised to call me as soon as he made his decision. As I was leaving, his name, which had seemed somehow familiar, clicked into place. He was Curt Stern, the geneticist who in the 1920s had made important genetic discoveries using fruit flies. I knew there were more experienced applicants for the position, but I wasn't really surprised when he called me to say I could have the job. Nor was I surprised at all the times he sent me to the library to look up German books and journals.

Just before I started working, I had found a room in an apartment with two other girls. It was a tiny room, barely big enough for a bed, with a sloping ceiling, but I liked the apartment and moved in. The two girls were Barbara and Eve. Barbara was fanatically fussy, spending hours keeping the kitchen immaculate and getting hysterical about any little spill. Eve, on the other hand, was a treasure. She was always rushing off to work or play tennis or write poetry, yet always seemed to have time to let me know she cared about me. I finally felt like I had a friend.

The Red Clogs

The red clogs. I remember them. I saw them when I first came to Berkeley, that summer of '69. I looked at them in the store window and wanted them. Had to have them. Ellen had clogs, back at school in New York. I liked just about everything Ellen had. Her purple clothes. She dyed everything purple, even her sheets. So I dyed everything purple. Her clogs were blue. But I wanted mine red. After looking at them in the window for a week, I bought them. Why not? I could do it. I had just gotten a job. Never mind that I had the rent to pay, and it would be a month till I got paid. And I had to send Steve $75 so he could fly out to visit. A week before I got paid, I ran out of money. So I went on a brown rice and beans diet. It was very cheap.

I had changed that day that I got the shoes. I was no longer an ordinary person who wore ordinary shoes. I was someone who wore red clogs. It was a big difference in my life. I was special now. They consoled me on those long boring days in the lab. Long hours during which I could barely keep my eyes open. Was it from the boredom of the dull routine that I was falling asleep, or was it from the ether I was using to anesthetize the flies? I didn't know. But the red clogs, they perked me up. It was fun just walking in them. The tap-clap, clippety-clack they made sounded brisk, efficient, self-assured. Like someone who was doing an important job was wearing them. It fooled me, and I forgot my tiredness. I was a very special, important person. A person with red clogs.

Once I started getting my salary from this job, I had more money than I had ever had before, for it paid generously. By the time this ten-month position ended, I had managed to save several thousand dollars from my paychecks.

Steve graduated from Stony Brook the semester after me and moved to Germany to join his Brooklyn friends, who had formed a successful band there. As soon as my job ended, I also decided to go to Europe. I hitchhiked all over the British Isles and Scandinavia during the summer of 1970, while the band was cutting an album. One time, in Wales, I got a ride with a bunch of Gypsies. When the recording was finished, all the band members except Steve decided to go to India. They were into a spiritual guru there, but Steve and I couldn't stomach their holier-than-thou attitude. We went to stay with Steve's art-student friends in Arnhem, a small Dutch town near the German border. I was looking at a book of African art there one night. The masks mesmerized me.

"Let's go to Africa," I said to Steve.

Exploring

Into Africa

I woke up to the sound of "Silent Night" playing on a battery powered radio. It was Christmas morning, 1971. I noted the incongruity, somehow appropriate, of hearing Silent Night playing here, in the middle of the jungle, in the middle of this tiny island in the middle of Lake Victoria, in the middle of Africa. That was the only manifestation of Western civilization here besides my fellow teacher Jane and me. But now, decades later, what I find really strange is that I remember so little about that day and the people around me. Oh, I know I had come there because one of our students at Bwanda Senior Secondary School on the Uganda side of the lake had invited us there to spend Christmas with her family. I do remember taking a few steps into the thick jungle just outside the hut and seeing monkeys and parrots, only to have a family member come anxiously searching for me. I was so used to the freedom of going where I pleased while I had been traveling. I was not used to the people's concerned solicitude. And I'm sure Christmas dinner was matoke and chicken in a sauce of ground peanuts with onions and tomatoes, but that was dinner more often than not in Uganda. One was always smelling the fragrant aroma of the matoke bananas, a big pile of them wrapped in banana leaves, steaming for hours.

It must have been that the multitude of events of the last year had completely filled me, that there was no room in my memory for more. Now it amazes me. How could so much have happened in just one year? How could my life have changed so drastically, irrevocably, in one year, and my vision of the world been so altered?

One year earlier, Christmas Eve 1970, I was alone in a hotel room crying. In the morning I fought down my depression, determined to go out and enjoy the city. After all, during the last months I had discovered what a thrill it was to come to a totally strange city in a new country and explore it. I had loved London, Amsterdam, Copenhagen, Oslo, Athens, Jerusalem. I wasn't going to let the present circumstances deprive me of that pleasure now, in Lisbon. Anyway, I realized that I had set my expectations too high. How could I have thought that Steve, who could not be trusted to find his way from his family's home in Brooklyn to my parents' house in Queens, who would more likely than not take the wrong subway and wind up in the Bronx, how could I have expected him to meet me at this rendezvous?

"No boats to Ethiopia. Arriving Lisbon Dec. 24. Meet me or leave message with address at American Express office."

I had wired him from Israel to Germany. As we had agreed, I had gone to Israel not only to visit my birthplace and my grandmother for the first time since I'd left as a child, but also to see if I could find a boat to take us to Ethiopia. I had spent a couple of days scouting the port in Eilat. None of the boat captains, mostly of commercial fishing vessels, whom I had talked to would consent to take passengers. That left only one way for us to get to Africa. The usual cheap way, the route from North Africa across the desert by Land Rover, was closed to me. Even though I had a US passport, I had "Israel" stamped above "birthplace," and at that time no North African country would have let me in. So there was only one way to go on our limited means. We had discovered that there was a boat from Lisbon, Portugal, to Luanda, Angola, for $110.

So I had written the telegram, and he wired back that he was leaving for Lisbon. I took a flight to Paris, then spent the next day and night on a train crowded with gigantic jugs of wine and Portuguese workers heading home for Christmas. But when I arrived at American Express, there was no Steve and no message. It was a very lonely Christmas Eve.

It was early afternoon the next day, after I had spent a

pleasant morning sampling some delicious Portuguese snacks, that I discovered the unbelievable: There were two American Express offices in Lisbon! I ran to the other one and breathlessly collapsed into Steve's arms at the entrance. He had been waiting there the whole morning, had just found out about the other office and was starting on his way there. After a happy, hysterical reunion, we spent the rest of the day comparing our favorite Portuguese pastries. The little custard tarts, we both agreed, were the best. The next day we bought our boat tickets: Lisbon to Luanda, twelve days, 6,000 miles.

We had a few days before the boat left so after we got our visas for Angola and several other West African countries, we went hitchhiking around the rugged southern coast of Portugal, spending New Year's Eve at a little inn at the very tip, cuddling and listening to the wind and rain howling outside.

Finally the day came, and we got on the ship. It was then that we discovered why the passage was so cheap. It was used mainly for transporting Portuguese soldiers to Angola, which at that time was still a colony, though struggling to be free, hence the soldiers going to fight the rebels. We were very naive, and completely ignorant of and unprepared for the political situation of our destination. Most of my knowledge of Africa was derived from Tarzan movies and my attraction to African art. I also knew it was a very big place. I had copied a small map of Africa from an atlas and kept it with my passport, just so I could keep the different countries and their locations straight.

And so we set sail. Twelve very languid, lazy days. I spent hours, day and night, watching the water, forever changing, forever beautiful. We watched the dolphins swimming alongside. We were in a never-never land. Time seemed as endless as the ocean.

I slept in a big cabin with several Portuguese women and their children. The women were always screaming at the kids, and it drove me crazy. One night, after a particularly upsetting scene in which the woman in the bunk below me kept hitting her little girl on the head with her shoe, I couldn't stand it any more. "Stop it! Stop hitting her!" I screamed, knowing she couldn't understand English, and ran out. I sneaked into Steve's cabin, hoping no one would notice me if I lay real quietly behind the curtains of his bunk, but the next day the steward gave me a stern warning not to try it again.

The food on board consisted solely of potatoes, very dry fish fillets, soda crackers, and wine. After a few days of this fare, we started longing for some fresh fruits and vegetables. We looked forward to our brief stop at the Cabo Verde Islands. The name suggested a lush green paradise, and we envisioned it filled with tropical fruits. After we disembarked, we asked our way to the marketplace. What was pointed out to us turned out to be an empty square. We asked where the food was, and someone came bringing two small bunches of bananas. One was brown and looked half rotten, the other green and unripe. In our desperation we bought both. We headed back to the ship but were followed by a crowd of skinny, shouting children. They were loudly, insistently begging for the bananas. We gave them the brown bunch and took the green ones on board, figuring they'd ripen during the trip. It was many months later that I happened to read a magazine article about the prolonged drought and famine on the Cabo Verde Islands.

The rest of the trip passed, with the only other memorable event being the crossing of the equator and the prime meridian. As the captain announced, at the same time we passed zero latitude, we were also passing the point of zero longitude. Although it was just an arbitrary designation, it gave me some satisfaction to know that I was in a truly unique point in space.

Steve and I had lots of time to talk. It was fortunate that we had this time to ourselves, for it helped form a strong bond between us that helped to see us through the months ahead. We realized that we were embarking on an adventure from which we might not emerge alive and accepted that fact. Ahead of us lay all kinds of dangers, we were sure: lions, poisonous snakes, crocodiles; but it was all part of the adventure. How mistaken we turned out to be, for I never saw a single lion or crocodile in Africa, and only two snakes, one of which was a dead one on the road. Yet death did come looking for me one day out of the blue African sky, and I held its cold hand. But I could not have guessed the real circumstances then, on that boat, as I tremulously waited for the adventure to begin.

We talked about what we would do once we reached Africa. We thought we'd try going east to the Congo, or try to get a boat to one of the West African countries. We had no cameras; I wanted to remember everything in my mind.

We finally reached Luanda. As I walked down the gangplank, I felt like I was descending into a sauna. It was so hot and humid. The next thing I was aware of was the most beautiful woman in the world crossing in front of me. She was gone so fast I had only the briefest impression of a great harmony, of a face seemingly carved out of ebony, serene and unhurried, surrounded by the bright pattern and colors of the cloth wrapped around her; then she was gone. Yet she had delivered a silent message of reassurance to me: I had come to the right place.

We spent a couple of days camping on the beach in Luanda, gorging ourselves on mangoes, papayas, pineapples, coconuts and avocados. I remember my first time at an African marketplace, surrounded by colorful fruits and vegetables and hundreds of dark faces, white eyes staring relentlessly at us. The second morning on the beach, we woke up to find a camera hovering over our faces, snapping away. We had been discovered by the local press. Though it was annoying, we found the reporter to be a valuable source of information, and he quickly filled us in on what was happening in Angola: namely, war. We had noticed that people seemed afraid. When we had approached anyone to ask directions, they ran away. Once I had noticed a child's beautiful bead necklace and had gone closer to get a better look, but he had run away in terror.

We found that the way to the Congo was closed to us, for there was fighting along the Congolese and Angolan border. Nor could we take a boat up north to West Africa, for none of those countries had any relations with Angola now. The only country which did was South Africa. In fact, the only road out of Luanda open to nonmilitary vehicles was the road to South Africa. This was quite a setback to our plans. We had no desire to go to South Africa. We wanted to get to the Congo or West Africa. Still, we could cross South Africa, go up north to East Africa, and from there to the Congo. It would mean a detour of thousands of miles, but there was no other way. The next morning, after glancing at the front page newspaper article, "Hippies Invade Luanda," we found the road going south and started hitchhiking.

As I mentioned previously, Steve was very gregarious and had a way of drawing people to him like a magnet. There was an openness about him, a vulnerability that made all kinds of people trust him, open up to him, and want to take care of him. This was partially an act he had developed to make people let down their guard, for he was not as naive as he appeared to be. But it was mostly true; he was very dependent on people and really needed them.

The result of this trait was that we were always meeting unusual and interesting people and making friends. More often than not, they would invite us to stay with them and would give us names and locations of friends and relations to look up farther along on our route.

Steve had a related quality that was not as well suited to traveling. As mentioned earlier, he had difficulty keeping track of what was his. He was always losing his things and picking up something that didn't belong to him, often unaware of his action until someone pointed it out. His close circle of friends at home accepted this trait as a matter of course, as one would accept any friend's disability, and just kept an eye on their belongings when he was around. Now, as his traveling companion, I had to make adjustments. I carried our passports and money, and checked to make sure he hadn't left something behind or taken anything he shouldn't, and I always made sure we were on the right road. Steve, on the other hand, was the one who did the talking, made friends and connections for us and entertained our hosts while I was content to watch and listen. This system of dividing the responsibilities worked well for us in our travels.

So it was that we headed for South Africa. Now although this was only 1971, South Africa was known even to ignoramuses like us as an unpleasant, racist place where people practiced a severe form of segregation which they called apartheid. In other words, I was expecting to find a place like the South. Two years earlier, during the Christmas break, we had driven down to Florida with some of Steve's friends. We'd been arrested and questioned for several hours in a police station for no other reason than that the boys had long hair. They had compared us to "niggers," and I realized where the term "pigs" had come from. They let us go only after one of the boys thought to mention that his father was a lawyer.

So we were expecting something along that line from South Africa. We were not prepared for the shock ahead. First, we went through Southwest Africa, a hot dusty place that reminded me of the Old West. The women wore long full dresses, sort of like pioneer women. I don't remember exactly at what point we realized that this was not going to be anything familiar. But very soon after we entered South Africa, we realized that these people were not cruel, or stupid, like the cops in the South; they were insane. I also realized that we had

91

to get out of there quickly, for I felt like I couldn't retain my own sanity there. It was like the twilight zone, a science fiction country. The people seemed unreal. It was all a surreal caricature, and a heavy depression descended on me.

First, contrary to our expectation, the white people did not treat us badly because we were "hippies." In fact, we were treated like royalty, or to be more precise, like the ambassadors from another culture that they saw us to be. As soon as a car would pick us up—and we never had to wait hitchhiking here, the first car always picked us up—we would be given a speech about how the rest of the world misunderstood them; how the natives here were treated better than any other place in Africa; how the natives here earned more than in any other place in Africa; how the Europeans had to be in charge here, otherwise the blacks would kill each other off. We would inevitably be invited to their homes to have dinner with their families and to spend the night. They would drive up to their mansions, and they were all mansions. I learned that the standard of living here for whites was much higher than in the US. We would be served a fine dinner by a barefoot houseboy in rags, while our hosts discussed the inferiority of the African people. After our hosts retired, we'd sneak out into the back yard. There'd be a tiny shack there where the servants lived with their ragged children.

"How can you stand it?" we'd ask.

"We're waiting," they'd say. "Another ten, fifteen years, things are going to change then, you'll see."

This was something I couldn't understand. How can you wait fifteen years for something? I felt I could not stand this place another day. Yet we heard the same thing whenever we talked to any African, whether it was people on the road or the guy filling up the gas. Steve, as I said, was always talking to people, and so we found out about the ID cards, the danger of being caught away from home after curfew, the prisons where you could be detained for an indefinite amount of time without charges, people disappearing and never being heard from again. When we got to Johannesburg, we saw many strange sights in the city: a beautiful large bank with a fancy columned entrance, and in the back, a tiny dark entrance with a line of Africans a block long, waiting to do their banking. There would also be a long, long line of Africans waiting for the little dilapidated bus to take them to their homes at the end of the day, while the Europeans drove home in their Mercedes.

I guess it was the incongruities I saw and the blindness of the people that bothered me. The people there did not see what was in front of their eyes. Instead they made up a fictional reality which they anxiously tried to preserve and sell to us. It scared me that people were like that. I knew people could be stupid and cruel, but so self-deceiving and blind, that was a new one for me.

We raced through as quickly as we could, declining our hosts' invitations to tour the game reserves, desperate to leave this nightmare behind us. We only stopped in Johannesburg and Pretoria to get visas for the East African countries which still had relations with South Africa. We had thought traveling through Africa would be slow, but one week and 3,000 miles after we left Luanda, we exited South Africa.

We were not anyplace pleasant yet, however. We were in Rhodesia. We didn't stay in any towns but headed straight for a place we had heard about, the Zimbabwe ruins. We camped out in the shelter of the tall walls of the ruined city. These walls had been made by fitting the stones together without any mortar. The walls had held for thousands of years, the work of an ancient civilization. For us they were a confirmation of the beauty and culture of the people of Africa. The solid coolness of the walls soothed us after the lies of South Africa.

As we were preparing our camp the first evening, a tall African man approached. He was the guard here, he said, the sole person in charge. We asked if we were allowed to camp there. "No," he said, we weren't, but it was OK with him. He liked company. Thus we stayed for several days, content to rest there. In the evenings he'd come to our campfire, bringing a skin full of a milky sour beer. We asked where he came from.

"I'm a Zulu," he said, "from Durban."

We were surprised. Durban was a thousand miles away.

"How did you get here?" we asked.

"I walked," he said nonchalantly. Thus we heard what would soon be a familiar story. We had assumed, because the only people we had seen so far with cars were whites, and there were no intercity buses, that Africans didn't get around much. But especially when we were in East Africa, we noticed the number of travelers on the road, walking, hitchhiking. It was customary to give the driver a small fare for the lift, so truck drivers made an extra income by giving rides. We found that many people had traveled widely, some to find a better place to work, some to visit relations, some to see a famous witchdoctor. The guard told us that he was a witchdoctor.

"I can give you medicine," he told me, "for having a baby."

"I'm taking medicine for not having a baby," I said. He shook his head sadly. Those Mzungus, (white people) he seemed to be saying to himself, sure are strange.

After several days, we left. We crossed into Mozambique in the evening. There were soldiers everywhere. As in Angola, there was fighting in Mozambique. We reached the shore of the Zambezi River at night. It was incredibly hot. We camped out in our light sleeping bags and were devoured by mosquitoes all night long. We weren't worried about malaria, for we had been taking our preventative pills, but it was impossible to sleep. The ferry crossed the river at 7 o'clock the next morning. The sun was already hot, the temperature already reaching towards 100 degrees. We were not going to stick around any longer than that in Mozambique. We got a ride on the other side and gratefully felt the Land Rover climb up into the cool Malawi plateau.

Arriving

We reached Blantyre, Malawi, in the evening. We were happy, for we felt that we had finally reached Africa. We were no longer in some white colonial country, but in the real, black Africa. We drank in the musical sounds of Swahili around us, and checked in at the government rest house. This was a cheap hostel we had heard about where Africans stayed when they traveled. We were surprised at how crowded the place was. In the women's bathroom, the women all stared at me when I took a shower. Maybe they had never seen a naked white woman before.

We retired to our rooms. It got dark, and tired from our day's trip, we went to bed. Just as we were dozing off, we were suddenly awakened to the insistent sound of a drum calling. The sound was irresistible. We quickly got dressed again and went outside. There, in the square made by the surrounding buildings of the hostel, a large circle of women was gathered around a young boy, who was drumming. The women were singing and dancing around the drummer. It is hard to describe the beauty of that scene, which seemed to me to be there especially to welcome us to Malawi. The drumming, dancing, singing, each in itself was so pure and bold and clear, and together they seemed almost too good to be true. I felt incredibly lucky to be there.

Later, when the drumming and dancing was over, and we were in bed in our room, a different kind of music drifted in through a window. It came from a bar across the street, and this was no jungle drumming. It was modern music, featuring electric guitars and brass instruments, and was being played on a record player. As I mentioned, Steve was no stranger to music, having played it most of his life, and played electric guitar in a jazz-rock band himself, but this was different from anything either of us had ever heard. The guitars were bouncier, the rhythm more complex, doing tricks and turns no Western music did. Exhausted, Steve grumbled about the need for sleep, but I didn't mind it playing all night. I closed my eyes to see the dancing, playful notes, and was happy.

In the morning we found out that there was to be a big welcome in town for President Banda, who had just come back from a trip to England. We decided to go watch the festivities. Downtown was packed, a sea of thousands of people with Steve and me being the only white faces in the crowd. We managed to see Banda giving his speech. He seemed to be staring directly at us, or was it just my imagination? Suddenly, a group of dancers started performing. They were the same ones we had seen last night. So that's why they had been there! They had been brought in from their villages to welcome Banda to Malawi, not us. Last night's performance had just been a rehearsal.

Afterwards, we went to the market to buy fruit, and Steve invited some guys he met there to our room. I made some tea, African-style, boiling the tea leaves and adding powdered milk. They rolled a fat joint in newspaper and shared it with us. The best ganja in Africa, they said, grew here in Malawi. We asked about the music coming from the bar. That was Congolese music, they told us, so named because that's where it started, but nowadays much of it was also recorded in Tanzania. We told them that we longed to stay in the countryside, away from the city. They said it was possible to rent a hut from some of the fishermen who lived by Lake Malawi, and told us where to find one.

We arrived there in the evening. The fisherman was a Moslem and lived with his two wives right on the shore of the lake. Each of the wives had a hut, and there was an extra one where Steve and I stayed. The mosquitoes were terrible at night even though there were mosquito nets over the cots. Also, there were ants. They were huge and got into everything. In the morning, as I looked at what little remained of the underwear I had left near my bed, I realized that they also *ate* everything.

The sun had just risen, and I took a walk in the glowing morning air. Suddenly a beautiful red and green bird flew out of the bushes near me, and the sight filled me with a wonderful contentment. I took a swim in the lake. I was delighting in its clear warm beauty when I noticed something strange in the water near me. The fisherman had assured us that there were no crocodiles in this part of the lake so I wasn't worried. Just then, I saw the head of a hippopotamus emerging out of the water. He was enjoying the lake beside me.

One of the wives served us meals. Breakfast consisted of cooked cornmeal, called nsima, and tea. Lunch and supper were nsima and fish in a delicious sauce of onions and tomatoes. The younger wife was only seventeen but was very unhappy because she had not conceived after being married a year. She was going to visit a witchdoctor who lived nearby. We asked if we could come along, and they agreed. As we walked to the witchdoctor's hut, they told us that he was very powerful. He could fly. He was originally from Mozambique, but one night he had simply flown over the water to the Malawi side and had stayed here ever since.

There were two unusual things that struck me as soon as I saw the man. One was his eyes. They were a bright red. They could be bloodshot from drink, I thought, or maybe some infection has caused the capillaries in his eyes to burst. The second thing was more subtle and less explainable. He was wearing pants made of a thick, canvas-like material. They were a dull greenish-gray color and looked new and clean. Straight across each knee, however, was a tear. Both tears were identical and were sewn with a fine red thread in neat, perfectly even stitches. Of course, there was nothing unusual about his pants being torn, or mended, but there was something there that didn't make sense. For one thing, the pants were of such a heavy material, and the thread was so fine; it didn't seem possible that the stitches could hold. And then, the tears were so dainty and neat, and so identical, as if they had been planned, or even cut. And the stitches, they were too particular and even, like embroidery, but there was nothing decorative about the pants, or the man. He gave the young woman some herbal medicine. I left with an odd feeling I couldn't quite put my finger on. Steve, I found, had the same observations and feelings.

In the evening, Steve and I sat on a mat by the water's edge, talking in the growing darkness. Suddenly, a massive shadow rose out of the water, directly in front of us. Steve gave a loud scream and ran into our hut, but I sat mesmerized at the sight of the huge hippo as he slowly ambled away. The fisherman and his wives were in stitches over Steve's panic. "The hippo won't hurt you," they laughed. "Just be careful he doesn't step on you." Apparently, there was a family of the animals living in the reeds next door, and thus they were a very familiar sight here, no more frightening than cows. Many years later, I read that hippos can be dangerous and have been known to kill people, but our hosts were not afraid, and seemed to coexist peacefully with them.

We spent another uncomfortable night with the ants and mosquitoes. In the morning our host noticed our discomfort. Farther up the lake, he said, was a place with no ants, no mosquitoes. He told us to go to the town of Monkey Bay and ask for a man named Kenny Nyenyembe.

Zambo to Dar

Of all the people and places I came across in Africa, Kenny is the person who stands out, and his village will always be my favorite place. We found Kenny in Monkey Bay, and he and Steve clicked instantly. They were like kindred spirits who quite by accident had managed to stumble into each other. He invited us to stay with him and his wife in nearby Zambo, and we did.

We spent about two months there. We stayed in Kenny and Maggie's two-room hut. It was a typical mud hut, like the 20 or so others like it in the hamlet. It took over an hour to get there by foot along a narrow path through a dense forest where monkeys chattered at you. The path climbed first up and then down steep cliffs to the inlet. Or else you could get there by dugout canoe. There was no road.

Maggie was pregnant with their first child. Kenny told us how Maggie's former husband, jealous that she had left him, had hired a witchdoctor to put some bad medicine on them. He and Maggie had traveled all the way to Mombassa, Kenya, over a thousand miles away, to seek out a more powerful witchdoctor who had counteracted the spell.

I remember the dances in the evening. Kenny would take out his accordion—some of the keys were broken—and play Congolese music. "Tambala tatu, three tambala, three tambala," he'd cry, for that's how he liked to make his money, unlike the other men in Zambo who fished and sold their catch in Monkey Bay. He played his accordion in the evening, and people would pay to dance; three tambala, three pennies a dance. Maggie would be making and selling mandazi, the slightly sweet bits of dough giving off a delicious fragrance as they deep fried in the peanut oil over an open fire. Everyone else danced, the men trying to outdo each other in acrobatics, the women swaying gently with their babies on their backs, the children sneaking a dance for free. I'd sit and watch with Steve, savoring the moonlight, the music, the dancers, the soft lapping of the water on the shore.

During the day Steve and Kenny would talk animatedly about music, their passion. Kenny had played with a band in the Congo and knew Franco and his OK Jazz band, and Dr. Nico, famous musicians in Africa. It would be many years before they became known in the West. He introduced Steve to the different African styles such as West African High Life and Congolese music. I wandered around the village, trying to learn the life there; helping put up the roof of a hut, learning to weave a mat, doing beadwork with the kids or going with them when they went to chase the baboons out of the cornfield; conscious every minute of how lucky I was to be there. In every colorful bird that I saw, every time I swam in the clear lake, I knew that this was a tiny bit of perfection in the world, in my life.

I felt perfectly content in Zambo, would have liked to stay there forever. But Steve was getting restless. He started missing things. Western things. Western foods.

One day he got a craving for cheese. Of course, there was no cheese in Zambo. The only dairy product there was the tinned powdered milk people put in their tea. But there was a store in Monkey Bay that had cheese. Steve decided he had to have some that very day.

It would take over an hour to climb up the little path to get to Monkey Bay. It was already long past noon. I was concerned that it would get dark before he could make it back. We had been warned not to attempt the trip in the dark. One could get lost in the forest or fall down the cliffs, and there were leopards who hunted there at night. I tried to dissuade Steve from going, but he was adamant. "I'll hurry," he insisted. "I can make it back before dark, and if I see in Monkey Bay that it's getting too late to get back on foot, I can get one of the fishermen to take me back in his canoe." Some of the fishermen

100

had gone there and were not expected back till evening.

So he went. Uneasily, I waited as darkness came. The fishermen came back without Steve. It got very dark. The moon would not be out for many hours. I imagined Steve stuck halfway between Zambo and Monkey Bay, groping his way in the dark. Kenny got a kerosene lantern. He was going to look for him. "I'll go with you," I said, rushing after him. I saw a big machete in his other hand. "For snakes," he said.

We started climbing up. I wasn't scared, for I felt secure with Kenny and his machete next to me, and the woods were so strangely beautiful in the dark. As for Steve, I couldn't decide if to be worried or angry at him, so left off that decision till we found him.

We reached the halfway point on the cliff. Directly below us was a tiny inlet, with two huts where just one fishing family lived. We could see the light from a fire down there. And then, as we stood there, we caught the faint but unmistakable sound of laughter, shrieks and howls of laughter.

I knew immediately that there could be only one cause for such mirth: Steve was there! Kenny called down to them and the fact was confirmed. We scrambled down and were met by the sight of Steve, bundled in a blanket, his clothes drying by the fire, entertaining his hosts with the story of his evening's adventure. It went like this:

After buying some cheese and a package of cookies at the store, he had realized he would not have time to make it back on foot before dark. Therefore, he had gone to where the canoes from Zambo were beached. As he approached the place, he saw that they were just leaving. He shouted to the men to wait, but they didn't hear him. He thought he could catch them by wading across the short distance, only to suddenly find himself in water over his head, with the cheese, cookies, and his money floating beside him. He managed to gather them all and splashed to shore. The canoes had left without seeing him. Fortunately, the canoe from the little inlet had not left yet, and Steve was able to get a ride with them.

After we all had a snack of soggy cookies and cheese, one of the men paddled Kenny, Steve and me to Zambo. The night's adventure was over. But we had another adventure in store for us shortly thereafter.

It was not long before the end of our stay in Zambo that we decided, mainly out of guilt for having had the luxury of basking in a tropical paradise for the past two months, but also partly to "get in shape," that we needed a physical challenge. Nothing too extreme. Just enough to make us feel that we had "done something" in Malawi.

We knew just the thing. Malawi had one mountain. It was not very high. Just a big hill, really. Kenny told us we could climb it in a couple of hours, rest at the top for a while, then come back down the same day. If we wanted to stay overnight, there was a ranger and cabin at the top. There were streams one could drink from. "Any wild animals?" Well, there were leopards and hyenas there, but they only hunted at night. They *never* attacked during the day. It was quite safe.

So we started early one morning. We had been trudging up the slope awhile when a young African with a big backpack came jogging up behind us. He was carrying supplies up to the ranger on top, he said as he passed us. "How much farther is it?" we shouted after him.

"About an hour," he called back and was gone.

It had been pleasant hiking in the cool morning air, but after a couple of hours we were nowhere near the top, and starting to tire. We then remembered that previous experience had shown that Africans had a very different sense of time and distance. Something "just over there" would be many miles away, and "just now" or "very soon" could mean hours or even days of waiting. Still, the morning wasn't over, we had most of the day ahead of us, and there was nothing to do but keep going. But it was getting hot, and we were getting very tired.

We kept on, and on, the sun now burning high above our heads. We finally reached a stream and gratefully had a picnic lunch on its banks, soaking our feet in the cool water. Then it was time to move on. We had gone a considerable distance. Surely it wouldn't be long now. We did seem to be getting higher. Maybe after the next ridge, we would be able to see the cabin at the top. But that ridge was deceptive. Just over it there was another to climb, and one more after that, and suddenly the shadows were lengthening, and the sun's rays cooling to a soft yellow. And then, could it be, it was actually getting dark! Where was the top? It was just over the next hill, but that was hours ago, and here we were, exhausted and staggering, wondering when the hyenas and leopards would start looking for their breakfast. Then, as it started getting really, really dark, we realized that even if we reached the top, we would not be able to find the ranger's hut in the pitch blackness of the forest that we now found ourselves in. We started running, stumbling, yelling for help, wondering if the hyenas and leopards could smell our fear. Then, gratefully, a light, a kerosene lantern swinging from the ranger's hand, he having heard our cries and come out to find us. Finally, the wonderful safety of the cabin.

We did not go down the mountain the next day. We could not move the next day, we were so sore, and were glad to accept the kind ranger's invitation to stay another day. We descended two days later, stiffly, painfully, all our muscles still aching. Fortunately it was quicker getting down the mountain than it had been going up. We headed back to Zambo.

Sadly, our idyllic stay in Zambo was coming to an end. Steve was restless and wanted to move on. I wanted to stay but was not yet ready to be without him. I reluctantly got ready to go, telling myself that somewhere in Africa I would find a place I could stay without Steve, who was talking more and more of India. At the thought of leaving Africa, I rebelled. I would not leave. I could not leave these gentle people, this beautiful place, this life that was so close to the nature I loved. No matter what happened, I would stay in Africa!

I made a trip to Lilongwe and bought Maggie some baby things she had requested: diapers, baby powder and lotion, Vaseline. It was another bright, perfect morning when we departed Zambo by canoe: Steve and I, Kenny and Maggie, who was in early labor and going to the clinic in Monkey Bay to have her baby. I took a last look at the village, so pretty and peaceful on shore. Knowing this place existed gave me the strength to go on, to face what was ahead.

Kenny gave me a letter to give to his brother in Tanzania. This brother had been President Banda's chauffeur, had taken part in an unsuccessful assassination attempt several years earlier, and had fled afterwards to Tanzania to a guerrilla training camp. Banda was considered a puppet of South Africa and was generally hated. We said goodbye to Kenny and Maggie in Monkey Bay, and Steve and I hitched out. In a few minutes we got a ride from a South African couple vacationing in Malawi.

A few miles out of town a police barricade was waiting for us. As soon as they saw the names on our passports, they told us to get in the police car. They told the people who had picked us up that they could go. Before they drove off, I managed to yell to them in a voice loud enough for our captors to hear, to notify the American Embassy of what had happened, adding our names.

We were taken to a police station and searched, and the letter was found. They immediately pounced on it, and it caused quite a stir. What were we doing in Malawi? What was our connection to Kenny and his brother? They were reluctant to believe that we were just tourists. I repeatedly mentioned the American Embassy, and they finally let us go, notifying us that we had to be out of the country in 24 hours. Furthermore, we were to report to every police station on the way to the border.

So we set off uneasily. We were worried about Kenny, fearing that the letter would set the police after him and that he would not get off as easily as we did. To make matters worse, he had been expecting a shipment of ganja, which grew along the north shore of the lake. It was to arrive by boat in Monkey Bay that very day. Would the police get him for that too? We were forbidden to go back towards Monkey Bay, so we couldn't let Kenny know what had happened. There was nothing we could do, but we still planned to visit his brother in Tanzania and let him know what had happened.

Our destination was Tanzania, but that leftist-leaning country had no diplomatic relations with Banda's South Africa-friendly regime, so first we had to make a long detour to Lusaka, Zambia in order to obtain our Tanzanian visas. As we were riding in the next car that picked us up, we were startled to see a man yelling and chasing after the vehicle. "Mr. Steve, Mr. Steve!"

He was waving and pointing down a path that led off the road. We realized it was the path to the Moslem fisherman's house. We hastily got out of the car and went to the hut. The fisherman looked happy to see us.

"A letter has come for you," he said, handing Steve an envelope.

Steve took the letter eagerly. Maybe it was from his Dutch manager. He was hoping his record royalties would start coming in, for so far we had been living off my savings. But his look changed to one of dismay. The letter was from his draft board in Brooklyn. He was to report immediately for his physical at his local board, for this was 1971, and the Vietnam war needed young men.

How had they managed to track him to this little mud hut in this out-of-the-way place in Africa? It was some time later that he found out his father had given them that address, for Steve and I had been writing our parents during our travels. Now, Steve dutifully wrote the draft board back, saying that he would like to comply with their instructions and was making plans accordingly. He would go to the nearest place where he could take the physical, which, this being East Africa, was the US Army base in Ethiopia. Since his means of transportation was hitchhiking, he estimated that it would take several months for him to get there. It was probably one of the strangest letters the Brooklyn draft board ever received, but even stranger was the fact that Steve kept his promise. Several months later, he turned up at the US military base in Ethiopia. They were so surprised by his request for an Army physical that they obligingly let him fail it.

That last night in Malawi, on the way to the border, we stayed at the house of some Peace Corps volunteers. They told us more about Banda's regime. Spies and government informants were everywhere in this small country. We had obviously been watched, since the police knew of our plans to leave Zambo that day. I remembered the day of Banda's speech. Was that when we had first been noticed and suspected because we were not typical tourists? Then there was the day a man had greeted me and asked all kinds of questions just as I was coming back to Zambo from Monkey Bay. I had thought nothing of it then, for people were often curious, but now I wondered who that man was, for he had not been one of the fishermen. We told our hosts what had happened, and they promised to go to Monkey Bay and find out what had happened to Kenny and to write us about it. We did get a letter from them weeks later, saying that Kenny had been arrested but then released, and that Maggie had a healthy baby girl.

We entered Zambia the next day and headed for the capital. Lusaka was the only place in Africa that I found totally uninteresting. I vaguely remember a lot of women sporting the latest styles from the West, miniskirts and Afros. We stayed at a Sikh temple, where travelers can always find shelter, and went to their chanting prayer session.

I'll never forget the big lorry that took us, along with its cargo of copper, from Lusaka to Dar es Salaam, over a thousand miles, its two drivers taking turns sleeping and driving for five days nonstop over the deep gullies of a road that had not been built yet. We hung on in back, jerked and rattled out of the dry savannas of Zambia into the lush green tropical hills and valleys of Tanzania, hanging on, delighting in the bright colors and waving to the Chinese workers who were building the railroad parallel to us. We were finally deposited, covered with a thick layer of red dust, in Dar es Salaam.

Dar seemed like a fairy tale city, the graceful arches of its pretty little white mosques glimmering toy-like in the sun, the many fragrances of the city's sidewalk vendors drawing us in. Cardamon-steeped coffee, coconut curries, red-spiced cassava, all beckoned lovingly. Raindrops of liquid-silver Swahili showered us as soon as we approached. Their meaning soaked into our skin through unseen pores. "Karibu," welcome. From storefront radios, a dozen playful rhythms swayed and seduced us. These lovely sights and sounds and fragrant smells, mixtures of African, Indian and Arab cultures, made it my favorite city in the world.

Strange Times

Island Rain

I was almost in view of the house, just approaching the outcropping of rocks around the final bend in the path, when I saw the lizard. There it was, motionless against the shimmering heat, just like that other time, the day Steve and I had rented the house from Abdul and moved in. I hadn't seen it since, though I always kept an eye out for the big, majestic three-foot-long creature, colored a gray yellowish tan like the ground, camouflaged so you wouldn't notice it till you were right on top of it, almost. Then, there it was, looking like it came from a science fiction movie set, sending little shivers through you. I had asked Abdul about it, but he just said to leave the lizard alone.

Suddenly it wasn't there anymore, though I hadn't seen it move. It had been like that the other time too. It just appeared, then disappeared, like an omen.

The strap of my basket was chafing my shoulder. I started walking again, thinking of the fish. I must get home and clean it before it started spoiling in the midday heat. I trudged down the dusty path, then up the final slope. I could see the house now. There it was, a bare rectangular brick house, surrounded by slender coconut palms. The front half of it consisted of a screened porch, leading to a hall which divided the back of the house into two small rooms. The thatched roof made it tolerable. It would have been too stark otherwise. But actually I liked it that way, stark and bare. I didn't want it to be too comfortable. I didn't want to stay here too long. I didn't feel at home here in Lamu, not like on the mainland. I missed the red earth, that wonderful rich red earth of Africa, so welcoming and comforting. I always felt at home there, no matter what happened. Here, the yellow-gray sand was a constant reminder that I was a stranger.

I felt a drop of rain just as I opened the screen door. I put down the basket, took out the fish and started cleaning it. It was raining steadily now. If I waited till it stopped I could make a fire outside. The rain never lasted more than half an hour, but I was too hungry to wait. I decided to cook the fish on the little kerosene burner we had bought, and after some time managed to get the stove to work. I cut up an onion and tomatoes for the sauce, added curry powder and the fish. I ate it with some cold cornmeal nsima left over from breakfast, rolling the cornmeal into little balls and dipping it in the sauce, like they did on the mainland.

I thought of the fishmonger who had sold me the fish in the market that morning. I always bought my fish from him. "Mvua," he had said, pointing up to the sky while wrapping the fish in newspaper. "Ndyo, mvua," I had replied, for of course it would rain, like it did every afternoon. I was becoming familiar with the polite, reserved friendliness of the island people, helpfully making polite conversation in Swahili, yet hiding themselves behind a social curtain that was as opaque as the bui-bui, the black veil that every woman on Lamu wore outside her home. It covered them from head to ankle, with only the eyes and feet showing.

"Why do you wear it?" I had asked Abdul's daughter.

"Out of respect for my father," Fatima had replied, noting that when she was in Mombassa, where she went to boarding school, she didn't wear it. Few women on the mainland wore them, and even the ones who did left their faces uncovered.

I had taken the fish and paid for it. The fishmonger was still trying to explain something, gesturing up at the sky, but I was unfamiliar with the words and gave up trying to understand. The sky looked brightly strange, like it always did. I was getting used to the surreal-looking sky of East Africa, to the strange cloud formations bathed in otherworldly light, to the sudden brief warm showers that bothered no one, to the glittering sun which quickly dried everything again.

I had decided to come straight home from the market and not stop to visit anyone. It was so easy to get hung up for hours in town, and I did so enjoy my solitude now that Steve had finally left. I just wanted some peace. These last few weeks with Steve had been unbearable. The six wonderful, intense months we had spent hitchhiking through Africa, so completely tied to each other, had strained our relationship, and we were getting on each other's nerves. He had been driving me crazy these last days especially. He could be cruel sometimes and knew how to make me miserable. I had wanted desperately for him to leave, yet was careful not to show it. If he felt that I wanted to get rid of him, he would stay just to spite me. So I had been patient and let his own restlessness drive him on, let him make the decision to go. He had left the day before yesterday, on the boat to the mainland.

It was still raining, so I put the dirty dishes outside to soak, and put some water on for tea. Steve was probably in Mombassa by now, looking for a boat to India. He said if that didn't work out he'd hitch to Nairobi and from there north to Ethiopia. He'd stop at the US Army base there and take his physical. Hopefully he'd fail it and then get a boat from Asmara to Saudi Arabia, and make his way to India from there.

The water was boiling. I stirred in the tea leaves and let them simmer a few minutes, African style, then stirred in the powdered milk. I remembered the mandazi I had bought in town, and took one out of the basket. The chewy chunk of fried dough was delicious with tea. I felt contented, just sitting on my verandah, watching the rain drench the palm trees. I had no desire to go to India. I never wanted to leave Africa. Mainland Africa, that is, not this place. I had my own plans. I would stay here a few weeks, then go on west. I'd keep going west through Uganda to the Congo. I had heard of a boat going down the Congo River, all the way to its mouth in West

Africa, an incredible journey of over a thousand miles. After that I'd get a job teaching in a school around there, in Gabon or Cameroon. I could get a job here in Kenya, I knew, but these last months had instilled in me a love of adventure, and I wanted to make this last great trip across Africa.

I poured some more tea and watched the droopy-leafed palm trees, their usually graceful trunks looking cold and naked as the rain continued to soak them. "This is a really long rain," I thought, and drank some more tea, and looked at the gray rain and gray trees, and listened to their gentle whisperings. After a while I realized it was getting grayer and dimmer, and with a shock I realized that night was coming, not with a final bright blaze of color as usual, but with a gradual darkening, for it was still raining. I went into the room in back in which my mat and sleeping bag were spread out, and crawled in and fell asleep to the sound of that gentle whispering. Sometimes in the night the whispering turned to a roaring, but maybe that was just a dream, because when I woke up, the whispering was still there, and when I ran to the window, I saw to my utter amazement that it was still raining.

I opened the back door and went out past the big mango tree to the latrine Abdul's wife had finished digging just a few days ago. On my way back I picked up the three mangoes that had fallen from the tree during the night. One of them would be my breakfast. Lamu mangoes were famous, for they were not ordinary ones. They were huge and especially delicious, and they weren't stringy like other mangoes. Nothing else seemed to grow here except these mangoes and coconuts.

I washed up with some of the water I had gotten from the well the day before, then put the bucket outside. Might as well let the rain fill it up. I brushed my hair and braided it. I made tea again, and put in lots of milk powder, and cut up the mango and ate the creamy golden slices slowly. I watched the rain outside. It didn't seem to change. There was hardly any wind, just a steady, gentle rain. The palm trees looked stoic.

They could take it.

Maybe this afternoon, when the rain stopped, I'd go into town and visit. There was the young English couple, James and Barbara, who had rented the beautiful old stone house in town. It was one of those old Arab style buildings with graceful curves and arches. They were waiting for an opportunity to buy a dhow, one of the old trading boats that made their way between the coastal cities. Steve and I had come to Lamu from Mombassa on a Somali dhow. That vessel had looked like it came from a thousand years ago, and we had been terribly seasick on the two-day journey. I never wanted to be on one again. But James and Barbara were planning to sail and live in one, trading in, among other things, the highly sought mangrove wood which they would buy in Saudi Arabia and sell up and down the coast. Barbara had just come back from Mombassa two days ago, where a doctor had confirmed her pregnancy. I wondered what it would be like for Barbara to live on a boat with a baby.

I envied Barbara, for I longed for a baby myself, but Steve had a fit whenever I mentioned the subject, so I had kept taking my birth control pills. Yet I so admired the African women with their babies tied in a bright kanga on their backs. The women didn't seem at all burdened by them, and the babies were always either asleep or looking at everything so sweetly wide-eyed. I never saw them fuss or cry, like babies at home. Why that was so was a mystery to me, together with how the mothers knew when the baby had to go to the bathroom. They didn't wear diapers, yet the kangas were never dirty or stained. Sometimes I would see a woman casually clean up after a toddler when he was playing naked on the ground, but I never figured out how this worked when the child was on his mother's back. When we had stayed in Kenny's village in Malawi, I had learned all about village life: how to weave mats and grind peanuts and dry fish and cook and even how to build a mud hut, but I never solved that mystery, and I never heard a baby cry there, even though there were quite a few babies. Were they just more content in Africa, like I was, or was it because they got to ride on their mother's back all the time? I resolved that when I had a baby, I would carry him on my back like that.

I had wanted to stay longer in the little fishing village. I had loved the life there. Kenny had even told me I could get a job teaching English in the school in the nearby town of Monkey Bay, but Steve was forever restless, and I wasn't ready to be without him then, and so we'd left. But I promised myself that I would get a teaching job somewhere else in Africa and let Steve move on without me.

And now Steve had left. Abdul too had said I could teach in the school here in Lamu, but this was not the right place. Still, I needed someplace to rest awhile. We had covered how many thousands of miles in the last few months? I was still tired from my bout with malaria in Tanzania, or was it from that shaky five-day truck ride from Lusaka to Dar es Salaam? Steve was too restless to wait. He constantly wanted to move on, to reach someplace with so-called "culture," India, or at least Ethiopia. I wanted to get as far away from "culture" as I could, to be totally immersed in the coutryside, for I loved the ever-present nearness of nature that was the dominant motif of life in Africa.

Originally, Lamu had seemed like a good place: an island off the northern coast of Kenya, as yet undiscovered by tourists. But it didn't turn out to be as I expected. All these women veiled. I found it depressing, oppressive.

"Out of respect for my father," Fatima had said.

"But what about you?" I had wanted to reply, "He doesn't seem to respect you, expecting you to live entombed in a shroud."

Instead I asked, "Aren't they uncomfortable?"

"Oh, yes," Fatima said, "they're so hot and stifling, and because we must hold the veil in front of our faces, we have only one arm free to carry things. It is very inconvenient."

They are insane, I thought to myself, to voluntarily suffer like this in a hot tropical climate. But then I thought of my mother's tight girdles and her ever-present high heels which had so deformed her feet that she could no longer walk in flats. Even her slippers had to have heels, and walking barefoot was impossible.

I washed yesterday's and today's dishes just outside the back door. Then I started to boil some rice. I'd have rice with fried eggs for lunch. I thought of the delicious meal Ali's mother had cooked the day before yesterday. The rice cooked in coconut milk. She had shown me how she grated the coconut, then had put it in a special basket sieve and soaked it in water till the liquid turned milky white. She had cooked the rice in it, then served the wonderfully aromatic grain with curried chicken.

I looked at the gray streaks outside. They were slanting at a slightly bigger angle now, I thought. The palm trees looked like tired old women, still tolerating the rain's abuse. Every few days Abdul sent a couple of young boys who scampered gracefully up the trees and cut down the ripe coconuts. They probably wouldn't come today.

Funny, I thought, how underneath their bui-buis, the women wore the brightest clothes I had ever seen. Neon oranges, lime greens, brilliant fuchsias and magentas, in screaming combinations with wild floral patterns and swirls. They took the bui-buis off at home, but if a visitor knocked, the women scampered off to hide. Even the prostitutes, Barbara said, wore bui-buis, and you could only recognize their profession by their red sandals. I had once seen several women wearing red sandals walking together, and wondered if they were prostitutes, and if other women had to avoid wearing red sandals in order not to be mistaken for one.

There were some advantages to the veils, Fatima had said. A woman was totally anonymous when she wore it. She could

117

go anywhere she wanted without being recognized. If a woman doubted her husband's fidelity, she could just follow him wherever he went, for the veil was so concealing that a man would not even recognize his wife. Sometimes men or boys would put one on for just that reason if they wanted to go someplace incognito. Teenage boys were especially notorious for sneaking into the secret women's ceremonies in a bui-bui, then bragging about it to their friends. For some women chose not to take off their covering inside, and no one would question them.

I remembered the time I had been invited to the women's ceremonies of a wedding. It was held in a large courtyard crowded with veiled and unveiled women, though who knew, maybe some of them were boys. The air was full with loud drumming and the heavy perfume of jasmine, for jasmine garlands were draped over everything and the smell was overwhelming. In the midst of the throng was the bride, a pretty girl of fourteen, her hair plaited in dozens of tiny braids and topped by a thick cap of jasmine blossoms. She sat propped between several large women and appeared as if drugged, for her eyes were closed and her face was a ghastly gray. At one point it was time for her dance. Two of the women rose, supporting the girl between them, and maneuvered her around in a slow circle. The bride never opened her eyes, her face showing no sign of life, looking more like she was about to attend her funeral than her wedding.

The rain was still coming down. I ate my lunch. I still had a lot of kerosene. I put some water on for tea, then rolled myself a joint from the bag of grass Steve had left, for he didn't want to travel with it. I didn't like to smoke it very often, for the strong African ganja made me too lethargic in the heat, but there really wasn't anything else to do today. The rain didn't show any sign of stopping.

I remembered how happy Ali had been when I had offered him some. "Nataka weedi?" I had asked. It was very hard to come by in Lamu, for marijuana wouldn't grow in the sandy soil here. He invited me to his house to have lunch with his family. I hadn't really spoken to him before that; we had just exchanged "jumbo"s in passing, but I had liked his open face and genuine happy smile, so unlike the usual masked ways of the islanders. His large kohl-rimmed eyes looked like they wanted to share a joke with someone. He was tall and gangly, and his palms and fingernails were hennaed like the women's.

He had a younger sister of maybe fourteen or fifteen, and a little one lying in a crib. Though she was three, she was unable to walk on her thin, undeveloped legs. His family didn't speak any English, so conversation was difficult, but they invited me to come again. I had asked about the designs the women hennaed on their palms, and Ali had offered to henna my palms and fingernails next time.

The rain, I noticed, was really quite lovely in the afternoon light. So translucent, not really a gray like I had thought, but silver. Many, many variations of silver, from heavy mercury to shimmering diamond. And the palm trees really liked the rain, I noticed now. Why, they stretched toward it, leaning to embrace it, letting it caress them ever so softly. I envied them their sensuous pleasure. I found myself shivering, and got up and got my woolen maroon cape from the back room. I had bought that cape in Berkeley, and treasured it. I languished gratefully in its soft warmth, while a gentle wind tried to make up its mind whether to stay or go. When it got dark I lit the kerosene lantern and made some more tea and put lots and lots of powdered milk in it, and the mandazi tasted so rich and chewy. I went to sleep perfectly content to have it rain forever.

In the morning it was still raining. It looked exactly like it had looked yesterday. A sudden thought flashed through my mind. It was a good thing this house was on a hill; I didn't have to worry about being flooded. The town also was on a slight incline. I decided not to think about the mile that lay between me and the town. I cooked a huge breakfast of scrambled eggs with cornmeal and and tea, but before I ate it I rolled another joint. This looked like it was going to be another day of watching the rain; might as well make it interesting.

I thought about Lamu and its people. This place had a sad history. I had heard it had been some sort of center for the Arab slave trade. Captives from the mainland had been brought here to be sold or await further shipment to Arabia. There was a thick wooden post in the market square, with a heavy iron ring embedded in it, where slaves had been kept chained.

People also said Lamu had been a center of magic. Some said it still was. They said that while the threads of life were mostly smooth in other places, here in Lamu they could be twisted and tangled. Was that a legacy of the sad days of slavery, I wondered. Did this place have a curse on it, the vengeance of mournful spirits?

I thought of the bui-buis. Why would anyone let themselves be subject to this hot, suffocating prison? A voluntary slavery, a giving up of one's power, one's individuality. For what? For the anonymity of not being recognized, the comfort of being protected? It seemed so incredible that this could happen in Africa, where nature still reigned. Why, just a few miles away on the mainland there was a tribe whose women walked proudly bare-breasted, barelegged, with just a short skirt of bead chains covering their hips. What had happened in Lamu? Why had women allowed this to happen to them? "Out of respect for my father." That answer wasn't good enough for me, and I didn't think it was just sexual modesty that made them wear it, either. I thought of Barbara's friend who had naively arrived in a very short miniskirt last week, attracting men's stares. Yet I saw nothing lascivious in the men's eyes. Their gaze was cold, contemptuous. "Have you no manners?" they seemed to be saying. "It may be a custom in your country to walk around half naked, but here you are our guest, and isn't it a worldwide custom to show some courtesy to your host, and not step on his traditions by brazenly breaking his laws? Your friends at least have made some attempt to meet us halfway by covering their arms and legs. But we will not be discourteous to you. That would be beneath us, for we, at least, have some manners." I had felt embarrassed for the woman, for all of the Mzungus, as white people were called, for we were all ambassadors here.

I sliced open another mango and made some more tea.

I remembered the story that Abdul's nephew, Abdulla, told over and over again while he and Hassan and I were playing cards, not understanding why I didn't get it, why I didn't laugh. He told of his trip to Mombassa, of passing those women in the short skirts working in their fields by the road. "Why, they wear nothing under their skirts, and when they bend over their hoeing, why, you can see the whole business." He thought this was hilarious, and couldn't understand why I didn't laugh, and repeated the joke while his friend Hassan squirmed in embarrassment. Poor Hassan, he was forever uncomfortable, caught in a tormenting grip of cultural confusion. I had met him at James and Barbara's house, where he had rented a room for a while, but he found life with the Mzungus intolerable and had just moved out to room with Abdulla. Barbara had told me that, like many young people, he had been attracted to Western ways and hung around Mzungus. Several months ago in Mombassa, someone had given him some LSD, and he had never really gotten over the trip. Now he was continuously torn between two cultures, and I found it disturbing to watch the pain in his eyes. I identified with it, had felt it myself, though I was not disabled by it as he was. He would often start a sentence and not be able to finish it, and I felt then that I knew exactly why, for there would be two ways his mind could go. There was the traditional African way of his family, and there was the new Mzungu way, and he was caught in-between, perpetually stuck. Abdulla's attitude was more pragmatic. "Sure, we like those nice things you

121

have," he said, "the cars and radios and airplanes. We'll take those things, but we'll keep our own ways."

The rain was coming down in sheets now. I could barely see the blur of the palm trees. There were no more eggs, but I suddenly remembered the bag of peanuts I had bought in town. Was that more than two days ago already? I got them out of the bottom of the basket. I smoked another joint, and ate some peanuts and another mango. I wasn't surprised that it was still raining when it got dark again. I lit the kerosene lamp, and wondered at the shadows it made, and the unseen shadows outside, and was grateful for the comfort of my sleeping bag.

I woke up to the feeling that something was wrong. There was something loud and unexpected in the air. It took me a few minutes to realize that the sound I was hearing was the noise of silence, that it was no longer raining. I jumped up and ran through the porch and out the front door and into the blazing sunlight and out to the palm trees and gazed a long time at all the shiny water surrounding my little solitary island.

The Visit

It was shortly after the floods, when the roads along the coast were still washed out, and there had been no mail for several weeks. He had written me that he was coming on his way to a physics conference in Holland, but I didn't get the letter. I had no idea he was even planning to come. He just appeared one day. He had flown in and was showing people a photo of me, asking where I was. It was Ali who guided him to the house of the English couple I was visiting. I had just bought a crab at the fish market and was walking it on a string. Suddenly, there was my brother, out of the blue, in Lamu. I took him to my rented house outside the town and cooked the crab.

His role had sometimes been to make me come home. Like the time I had run away to Boston rather than spend another summer working at my parents' ice cream store. They wanted him to go there and bring me back. He refused, for once not doing what our parents wanted. Now he had come to check on me in Africa. I had been there for six months and had written them effusively about the beauty of Africa and its peoples. Apparently this led my parents to conclude that I had completely lost my mind.

To his credit, he didn't try to make me go back. He just wrote our parents back a letter testifying that I was still brushing my hair and seemed OK. He only stayed a couple of days. He seemed restless, and took off to see the game reserves. I had already seen herds of zebras, elephants, giraffes, and many kinds of antelope in Kenya, for the road from Nairobi to Mombassa went through the largest game reserve. I preferred to rest from the many previous months of travel, so declined his invitation to join him.

The Speck

It was just a spot. A little speck, nothing more, in the blue sky, but I knew it was coming for me, though no one said it yet. It got bigger, and then the policeman confirmed it: It was coming for me. I wasn't surprised. Why else would there be a plane in the sky now, at this hour? The police plane, which should have come hours ago, in the morning, with the mail, hadn't come. I had desperately rushed for it, had raced out of my house, run all the way to the dock and paid a man to row me here in his boat, but it hadn't come. That's how things were here. Now in the afternoon, the speck which was not the police plane was coming for me. It landed. I asked the pilot if he was from the embassy. He was, and his instructions were to take me to Nairobi. I asked more questions, but he didn't know anything more. We took off immediately.

I guess I would have enjoyed the flight any other time. I remember flying over the mainland, flooded near the coast, passing over a herd of elephants. I wondered what I would find at the journey's end. Strangely enough, I wasn't anxious any more. I was rather calm. Was it the extra adrenaline in my bloodstream, or was it just the realization that there was nothing I could do, that somehow everything had already been decided, and I could only wait for what was inevitably to come?

When we landed, another man from the embassy was there. He shook my hand, and finally I could get my questions answered. The questions no one had been able to answer since this morning, when the Lamu policeman had found me and told me a telegram had come saying something about my brother being ill and I should come at once to Nairobi. That was all; he knew no more. But there was no way to get there by road. The coastal road to Mombassa was flooded. Small planes flew along the coast but there were no passenger flights scheduled that day from Lamu to the mainland. However, the police plane, which brought the mail, would come in an hour, if I could only catch it. And so I had raced, and waited.

And now he told me everything. Everything I had already guessed: the accident, a collision. My brother in the hospital.

"Is he conscious?"

"Off and on. He was able to tell me that he was on a curvy mountain road, saw another car approaching, and not being used to driving on the left, swerved the wrong way. The other driver helped get him to the hospital."

"What are his chances?"

"Not good. He smashed into the steering wheel, which crushed his liver. He had surgery, but there isn't anything one can do for that."

My brother's eyes were open when I walked into the room. I think there was recognition in them. And was it relief, when he saw it was me, or was that just my imagination? There was also a great sadness in his eyes, but before I reached the bed he drifted into unconsciousness, and never opened them again. I took his hand. The nurse told me to talk to him, so I spoke. I told him I would take care of him when he got better. He could come stay with me in Lamu to recuperate.

"Speak to him in your native tongue," the nurse said. But I had forgotten Hebrew. I stayed and held his hand. At some point the doctor came. I asked if there was any hope and learned that there wasn't. There was nothing they could do. He had internal injuries. His liver was too badly damaged. It was just a matter of time. How long? Maybe days.

It got late. The nurses urged me to go to sleep, offering me a sleeping pill. There was nothing I could do, so after a while I took it, telling them to wake me if he regained consciousness, or if there was any change in his condition.

In the morning he seemed the same. But after some hours I felt his hand get gradually colder. His breathing slowed down, and then there was what I knew was his last breath. It was a quiet transition; very quiet, yet unmistakable. It seemed so gentle and natural, and I knew that the cold hand I was holding was no longer my brother's. He had left his body.

The nurse hadn't noticed, so I told her. She summoned the doctors. They asked me to leave the room while they tried to resuscitate him. But as I waited in the hall, I knew it was a futile gesture. He was dead.

Hanan

Many people expected me to leave Africa after my brother died, but they didn't realize how determined I was, and how strongly I felt about staying. This feeling that had been growing stronger and stronger the last months was stronger than anything. I would stay, no matter what.

"I won't let his death take me away from here," I told myself. I had done what I had to do, automatically, mechanically making all the necessary arrangements with the embassy; meeting my parents in Ethiopia. But when that was over, I wanted to stay in Africa, where I felt so—what is the word—connected. To what? To the earth, to nature, to a way of life that seemed so real and beautiful to me. It sounds corny, but it wasn't as naive as it sounds. I had already spent more than six months in Africa. Steve and I had hitchhiked from Angola in West Africa to the eastern coast of Kenya, and only a minimal amount of that time was spent in cities, only long enough to get a visa to the next country. Most of the time we had been out in "the bush," and so I had learned to live without Western comforts, which I did not miss in the least. Even the discomforts seemed somehow right. Take the insects, for example. I'm not just talking about the butterflies, although there were many, and beautiful ones. At night, there were mosquitoes buzzing and feeding off you, and in the day, flies always on you, pestering you, and ants biting you. Sometimes huge swarms of flying termites would suddenly appear at night, leaving everything covered with their silvery discarded wings. Another week it would be some other insect swarming, enormous beetles or other weird creatures. In spite of their annoying ways, I loved them. I'd never known there were so many insects on earth, many more insects than people. I'd read that before, but here I experienced it. I realized we must have killed most of them in so-called civilized places. But here they still were found in abundance, and the air was alive with their different sounds, and it made me feel good. I could hear life in the air, always, the life of many things, not just people. The mosquito bites and annoying flies seemed a small price to pay for that. Even when I came down with malaria, and later hepatitis and hookworm, I had no desire to leave. I took the medicines and recovered, and stayed. Oh, some of my energy was gone. I decided not to go on with my journey to the Congo and down the Congo River to Cameroon. Instead I stayed in Uganda and got a job teaching in a rural school there.

I wonder, if he had known he would die young, would Hanan have lived his life differently? I'm sure he really liked his vocation as a nuclear physicist, and the interest he had in his field gave him a lot of satisfaction, but I think he gave up a lot in order to pursue it to the degree that was expected of him. Because I didn't matter, he sometimes would let down his guard when I was the only one with him. I saw him doing things he didn't let others in the family see, like the time in Portland he had run jumping all over the house, screaming hysterically about his parakeet's egg. I had felt then that all was not right with him. Then there was the time in LA when he punched a hole in the hotel room door. I think he was under so much pressure to make our parents happy by excelling that he had to let go of normal adolescent things like an interest in a social life or sex, and sometimes the stress came out in weird ways. His behavior seemed like a sign warning me not to make the same choices he was making in his life. I knew I would live my life very differently.

This accident was not Hanan's first. When he was two, my mother discovered him floating face down in a goldfish pond at a neighborhood cafe, completely blue. She ran screaming with him to her brother, who raced him to a nearby hospital. After several hours of artificial respiration, Hanan was finally resuscitated. Then when he was ten, he fell out of the back of a moving truck and was in a coma for several weeks, but again made a full recovery. Maybe the pressure he was always under was a factor in my brother's proneness to accidents. Maybe this stress also played a part in my susceptibility to illnesses, for in addition to the then-usual childhood whooping cough, measles, mumps, rubella, and chicken pox, I also came down with scarlet fever, diphtheria, and diabetes. Maybe these things were a legacy of the Holocaust and its effects on our parents, especially our mother. I think subconsciously, we felt we had to make it up to our parents. Outwardly, my brother was very successful, but I saw signs that he was not happy in his personal life, the time he told me of his depression being only one. I wonder if that last, sad look in his eyes was for the sorrow his death would cause our parents; or for himself, for not having gotten what he wanted from his life before it was suddenly over.

I also wonder, these many years later, what would have been if my brother had lived. We had never been close. The rift that started out as sibling rivalry widened as vast distances separated us physically, for since I started high school he had always been studying far away and I hardly ever saw him. Later, our divergent interests and conflicting values formed the chasm between us, for he adopted my parents' traditional views and was a dedicated academic, while I chose a path of freedom and adventure. Still, I did wind up becoming a scientist, so am like him in some ways. The last year or two of his life, we became a bit closer. I started writing him after I moved to Berkeley, and he wrote back from Yale, where he was assistant professor. I sent him a package of candles I had made and a woven blanket I had bought in Mexico. The next year he visited Steve and me when we stayed in Arnhem, Holland, bringing us matching shirts he had bought in Turkey, where he had attended a physics conference. He and Steve liked each other. Hanan told us how cheap things were at the bazaars in Istanbul. "I'll probably go there again next year and buy more stuff, and then I'll be rich," he said, and something about the way he said it made me think he wasn't happy with his life, but didn't know what to do about it. I think my brother and I probably would have become closer in time. How I wish he had lived, if only because it would have made such a difference in my son's life to have an uncle. For many years, Hanan regularly appeared in my dreams.

High Tea

I was recovering. I was getting better. My body was rid of the disease. My urine was a normal yellow again. I could move around. But there was something wrong. I was not the same as before. The joy in life, the excitement was gone. The colors were not so bright anymore. The sun seemed too strong as it beat down on me when I walked. And I had lost my desire for adventure, for travel. I was tired.

"Don't worry," said my housemate, "depression comes with hepatitis," and she was off to her class. For the first time I felt lonely in Africa. Here in this big house, I felt cut off from the nature I had felt so comfortable in.

I met George Tukay at the university pool where I went almost every day to swim, to lie in the sun. He said he had been watching me. Was I ill? I told him my story. I was recovering from hepatitis. I had been traveling for months with my friend Steve, who had gone on to India while I stayed in Africa. I told him of my brother's visit, and his sudden death, and my determination to stay despite it. I had just been passing through Uganda on my way to the Congo, intent on going by boat down the Congo River to Gabon or Cameroon, and getting a teaching job there. I had been curious about Makerere University in Kampala. What were African students like? I stayed in the dorms for a few days and learned a lot, from barkcloth worn to mourn the king's death last year, to Afros, the latest style from America. One thing they had in common with students everywhere: constant complaints about the cafeteria food. The cafeteria matoke was inedible, not anything like what they were used to at home. Matoke, the national staple food, consisted of plantain bananas wrapped in banana leaves and steamed for hours.

Then I found out I had hepatitis. By luck I had found a room in the house of a teacher who rented rooms to students, and thus I had a place to stay during my recovery.

George was from a northern tribe. He was 25. The college students here were often older than the average American student. Financial and family obligations often delayed college for the few who could go. He told me how, when Amin had taken over a few months earlier, soldiers had gone around attacking students, beating anyone who was not of the Baganda tribe, including him. Tribal identity is not something one can hide easily. It is evident in one's physical features. He walked me back to the house, and the way did not seem as long as it usually did.

The weeks went by, and George came to visit me at the house or meet me at the pool every day. The colors seemed brighter when he walked beside me. I was not so lonely any-more as we talked, and I found some comfort as he held my hand or as I laid my head on his shoulder. Yet there were huge distances between us, and high walls. Sometimes I couldn't stand him, times when he would say things that, if he had said them now, I would scream, "sexist! ageist!" But I just let it slide, for I was afraid of saying something that might drive him away, and of being lonely again. So I said nothing when he jokingly referred to my 28-year-old housemate as "the elderly spinster," or made some remark about how soon my breasts would start to sag. I was 23, and in Uganda, where girls marry young, that is already considered an old maid.

I still felt ill. Though I should have been getting stronger, I wasn't. I went back to the clinic, and they found I had hookworm. I remembered the flood in Lamu a couple of months back, when I had to wade daily up to my thighs in water in which I saw donkey dung and other sewage floating. Or maybe I had contracted it in Ethiopia, in all that unsanitary mud I had to slosh through. "Come back tomorrow morning for your treatment," they said.

I went home and told George. "People call that medicine 'high tea,'" he said. "Do you want me to come with you?"

"No, I'll go by myself," I said, knowing he had a class then.

The next day I went to the clinic. It was about a mile's walk. They gave me a milky liquid to drink, and I started back.

Something happened on the way. I realized that the medicine I had taken was hallucinogenic, for the sky was quivering and making me seasick. I was drowning in a hot sea of nausea as the sun and thick wet air pressed down on me and tried to push me down to the ground. The colors of the trees and flowers melted together and ran in streams into my face, my eyes, my throat. I was walking in slow motion, my feet sticking to the red earth, and after a long time, I was still in the same place. I spent many weeks walking back to the house. I don't remember much of that journey now, but I know it was hard.

Then I remember stumbling into my room. George was there, studying. "How was the high tea?" he asked, but I didn't answer. I was already sinking into a soft darkness.

I woke up after a long time. I felt a gentleness all around me. It was a feeling like, have you ever had it, when you were a child, sick with a fever, and then one morning you wake up and the fever is gone and you hear birds singing outside your window and your mother comes in and pulls open the curtain and you see blue sky and green trees? Well, it was that kind of feeling. I'm sure the birds were singing outside the window, though I don't remember it now. I just remember waking up with my head in George's lap. He was studying, holding a book with one hand, stroking my hair with the other. For a few minutes, everything seemed just fine in the world.

Bwanda Senior Secondary School

It had been a Catholic missionary school, but during Obote's rule all the missionary schools had been taken over by his socialist-leaning regime. Thus, St. Theresa's Senior Secondary School became a government school, and took its new name, Bwanda, from the small neighboring village a mile away. The nearest town was Masaka, about 15 miles to the south. Kampala, the capital, was 70 miles to the north. Bwanda was a girls' high school, a boarding school.

This being southern Uganda, the majority of the students were Baganda, but there were others from more distant tribes who spoke different languages. Some were Batusi from Rwanda, and were very tall. As for the staff, we were also a motley crew. The headmistress was a Catholic nun, a Muganda (singular of Baganda people). There was another Muganda nun, a lay Muganda man and woman, an Asian Indian man, two Batusi men who were twins, Jane, the English Volunteer who was my roommate, and me.

The school was largely self-sufficient. It lay surrounded by its matoke trees which supplied the staple food, matoke bananas steamed in banana leaves. The students also cultivated beans, corn, peanuts, tomatoes, onions, and a leafy spinach-like vegetable. They kept chickens as well. Most of the girls had come from farming families, so the extra chores were familiar.

I was nervous at the thought of teaching. I had no training or experience in it. All I had was a bachelor's degree in biological sciences, but that was enough to get the job here where teachers were in short supply. I had been assigned to teach English and biology to first and second year students. I, who had always been scared to talk to people, was supposed to get up in front of a group of teenage girls, some of them almost as old as I was, and teach them. The thought was terrifying.

But, as it turned out, it didn't go badly at all. This was not due to any newfound talent on my part but just to the favorable circumstances. The most favorable one being that no one questioned my ability. The fact that they had an American teacher made the students feel privileged, and thus to them I could do no wrong. I soon realized that I too was fortunate to have this unique experience, and so I relaxed and had a good time.

Not that all the girls were model students, nor were they eager to learn all the time. One of the main challenges was keeping everyone, including myself, awake on those hot, humid days. This was, after all, a tropical country where it seemed nature had intended all life to nap away the long afternoons. Sometimes a sharp clap of thunder would jolt us out of our daze as incredible black cloud formations would pass across the bright blue Uganda sky. After a few minutes of a crashing downpour, during which it was impossible to hear anyone talk, a dazzling rainbow or two would appear, and we'd go back to our schoolwork, feeling somewhat refreshed. On most days, however, the daily drenching would come in the form of a soft, warm shower, barely noticeable except if you were outside quietly making your way to a sheltering roof.

Yes, this was Uganda, in the heart of Africa, right next to the Congo, and as tropical as it gets. The equator passed 15 miles to the north of the school. I crossed it every time I made the trip to Kampala and back. As for the landscape, well, I couldn't have asked for a more exotic-looking place. The old Tarzan movies had been filmed here. There were thick jungles full of hanging vines and swinging monkeys and beautiful birds. Misty, surreal looking swamps, with their lovely papyrus reeds, and of course, the ever-present red earth under the bright green banana trees. Matoke, plantain bananas, were the staple food, but there were many more different kinds, just as there were dozens of different words for banana in

135

Luganda.

I taught in English, which the girls had already learned in grammar school. I, however, learned little Luganda. I had managed to learn some Swahili in East Africa, for Swahili, having originated as a trade language, is easy to learn. But Luganda, I found out, was too much for me; I never got beyond the beginnings of greeting someone. It is a very formal language, reflective of the intricate, formal Muganda culture. It took several minutes to greet someone correctly, with great attention paid to the proper inquiries after the various extended family members, crops, animals, etc. Variations in pitch further complicated things.

You would think that, at the very least, I'd learn all the students' names. But even this I could not master. What made it difficult was that each girl had many names, and would interchange these according to no system I ever figured out. Besides having an English name, she could use any of several African names: one or more given names, her mother's name, her father's name, a name describing circumstances of her birth, i.e., twin, phase of the moon or day of the week, nickname, etc. This made keeping track of grades rather difficult.

What did I teach? How did I teach? Well, after ascertaining that no one was going to check on me, that all I needed to do, officially, was to make sure they learned the major concepts needed for their qualifying exams (for this was still a British system where students had to complete certain exams before being allowed to go on), I looked at the teacher's guides and textbooks. These, of course, were incredibly dull. I realized my main task would be finding interesting things to do.

So we read stories, often in the shade of a tree outside. We would stop for words or concepts that were new to the students, and would discuss them, comparing notes on our different cultures. I remember the puzzled looks over the word "superstition" in *Tom Sawyer*, and the sudden gleams of understanding when I asked if they knew of any days, circumstances, or actions that some people said were either especially lucky or unlucky. I found myself inundated with a flood of anecdotes which the girls vehemently insisted were true. I didn't argue, for who was I to tell them differently? Why should I be the one to say what was true in their lives, I who was just a visitor here?

On the days when concentration was especially difficult, we played word games; hangman was the favorite. For homework I assigned them compositions, the topics geared to satisfy my curiosity more than any other consideration. "Write about your home, your family, what you eat for breakfast. Write a page, starting with the phrase: The most important thing for me to do after I finish school is . . ." I was surprised when so many, even the brightest, most eagerly inquiring student, the one whose hand was always up, completed it with ". . . to get married." I realized that these girls' families had gone to the trouble and expense of sending them here for an education, not for its own sake, but to enable the girls to marry well. For educated African men now wanted educated wives.

What did I teach in biology class? I vaguely recall a textbook, but all I really remember are the frequent field trips we took in the surrounding countryside, the girls telling me about the local flora and fauna, though I wasn't sure if their accounts of fifteen-foot pythons lurking in the bushes were true or added for dramatic effect. Yet, more and more I was realizing that I was the one who was learning here. For it seemed they were imparting to me something so rare and valuable: a knowledge of Africa. I, for my part, wasn't really teaching them English or biology. I was teaching them Western civilization, and I didn't like that task.

But we got along well. I guess my quiet, unobtrusive manner, which would have led to my being trampled underfoot as a wimp in a US high school, worked well here. I had no need to assert my authority, for it was never doubted. I was not only a teacher, I was a Mzungu, a white person. Those points were enough to put me on a pedestal, but I had the further advantage of being a member of that glamorous if somewhat odd tribe: American. To top it all off, I had the added ultimate status symbol of teenage girls everywhere: a boyfriend with a motorcycle. This was my friend Jim, whom I had met in Kampala and who was the one who had told me about the job opening at Bwanda. He was in the Peace Corps and taught at a nearby boys' school. He was a frequent visitor at our house, and I would often go riding on the back of his bike, for there was nothing quite like riding a motorcycle through the African countryside. During Easter vacation, we took a trip to Rwanda, roaring down little village paths, scaring chickens, delighting children, flying through a world that we shared with countless insects.

Every afternoon, after classes were over, the students would gather outside, bring out a couple of well-worn drums, and while one or two drummed, the others sang and danced. They sang beautifully together, often one girl doing the lead while the others sang the chorus or harmony. They had incredible voices, very clear and vibrant. Maybe the Luganda language's attention to pitch is what made the girls such wonderful vocalists. And the girls' different tribal backgrounds gave them a wide repertoire, for they learned and sang each other's songs, and even though I didn't understand the words, I've never enjoyed hearing singing more.

Although the students came from different tribes and backgrounds, there was always harmony in the school. I never saw any arguments or fights. I heard of one incident that to me embodied the closeness and cooperation among the girls. The headmistress told Jane and me that at the end of the previous school year, when the students were going home for the summer, one of them had given birth to a full-term baby during the taxi-ride to her home. She was a largely-built girl, and so had managed to hide her pregnancy from the headmistress and teachers. The other girls had all kept her secret so that she could finish the school year and not be sent home early.

My housemate Jane was an English Volunteer, which is the British equivalent of the Peace Corps. She disapproved of my method of having the girls exchange papers and correct each other's work. She also disapproved of my male friends, first George, a Ugandan, and then Jim with his motorcycle. There was one thing Jane and I agreed on, though. The school, in addition to providing us with our little cottage and a small salary for living expenses, also supplied us with a girl from the village to do our housework. Jane and I both found the idea of having a servant distasteful. We realized, however, that if we dismissed her, she would lose a hard-to-find source of income. We pondered this dilemma and finally decided to have her come once a week, sweep the floor and do the laundry, and go home.

Conditions in Uganda got worse. Idi Amin was getting more and more insane. At the school or in the village, life continued as before, but we heard stories from the cities of soldiers slashing women's legs with knives if their skirts were too short, and of plans to throw all the Asian Indians out of the country. The village taxi, which was the sole means of transport to Masaka or Kampala, started displaying a sticker on its windshield proclaiming love and support of Dada Idi. This was understood to be mandatory. One day while I was teaching, there was a commotion outside the school. I couldn't stop the students from rushing out. A man had been found dead on the path to the village, a spear through his back. There were rumors of government informants.

The headmistress told me that one of the teachers had inquired about the fact that Israel was listed as birthplace on my passport. This was 1972, and Uganda's relationship with Israel, its former supplier of arms, had grown very hostile as Amin became friendly with Libya's Gaddafi. As the school

139

year drew to an end, I realized it was time to leave Uganda. I made a trip to the capital to arrange my departure. For the first time in my life I understood what was meant by the smell of fear, for it was definitely in the air in Kampala. Getting a flight out proved to be impossible. When I came back to the school the headmistress said she would help. She told me to pack all my things and be ready to leave at a moment's notice.

I borrowed Jim's camera and cassette recorder, and during the next few days took pictures of the girls and made a tape of their drumming and singing. They also would be going home for the summer in the following days. I said my goodbyes to the students, the teachers, Jim, Jane.

One night the headmistress sent two of the students to tell me to be ready in 20 minutes. The village taxi would take me to the airport then. There was a flight of missionaries leaving for Frankfurt, Germany, and she had reserved a seat for me.

I was leaving Uganda, leaving Africa, for good.

"Come back to us," the girls had said. But I knew I would never come back. As much as I loved Africa, maybe because I loved it so much, I could never go back. For one thing, the change was too big; I could not go through it again, not twice in one lifetime. Also, I felt I owed it to this land that had shown me so much beauty, to do what should have been done by all those others who had come there throughout the centuries: leave it alone.

Besides, I could not bear to go back to what I knew would not be there anymore. For the saddest thing to me about Africa was how fast it was disappearing. Before your eyes you saw it transformed, quickly and irrevocably changed. So much lost and gone forever; the old ways, the beautiful places. Even while you were there, loving it, your heart was aching; it was going fast. How could I bear to go back to Zambo, to find tourist hotels where the children had danced in the moonlight? How could I go to Bwanda, to find the papyrus gone, the matoke trees cut down for a highway, and the girls gone to the city? I'd rather remember it in my mind and count myself lucky to have been there when it was still the way it was.

It was too dark to see the papyrus swamps as I drove by them for the last time, but their otherworldly beauty had become a part of me. I can still see them. Their dainty heads, the almost-human angles of the plants calling out from the mist, beckoning with their slender limbs, calling me to witness yet another of nature's works of art.

Postscript

Three weeks after I left, Tanzanian troops invaded Uganda. Some weeks after that, I received a letter from Sierra Leone. It was from Jim. Since Bwanda was near the Tanzanian border, there had been fighting there. Jim had been staying at the house of some other Peace Corps people when the shooting erupted. They stayed in the house for three days, the body of a dead Tanzanian soldier lying in the yard while the fighting continued around them. Finally a Peace Corps helicopter picked them up and airlifted them to the airport. All the Peace Corps were flown out of the country. One member had been shot in the head on the way to the airport. Jim was reassigned to a post in Sierra Leone.

I was relieved that school had already let out for the summer when this happened, and the girls had been home with their families. I enjoyed listening to the tape of the girls' singing for many years, but then, on one of my numerous moves, it was lost. I still have the photos.

In the years since I left, I've heard much troubling news from Uganda: fear and privation under Amin, violence, kidnapped child soldiers, sexual exploitation of women and children, a devastating AIDS epidemic. So much horror is numbing. I'm encouraged to hear that there are good people and organizations at work, and that there has been some progress.

The Insects

There were so many of them, and so many different kinds, and they would change with time. One night it might be the flying termites' time to swarm, fluttering by the millions, their transparent wings lying in thick piles on the ground in the morning. The next week it would be some kind of flying iridescent beetle, swooping everywhere, crashing into anything in its way.

Their presence was felt in the air, thick with their noise. Their hums, chirrups, buzzing, grating, chewing, the sound of their calls, the fluttering of their wings. It was always there. In the daytime, as sure as the heat of the sun beating down on an earth teeming with life, millions of lives, you knew they were there. For every one you saw, there were millions unseen, hidden, yet obviously there. You were never alone. They were there at night, the mosquitoes buzzing in multitudes, the ants eating everything left out for them. It was comforting, somehow, having them there. You were surrounded by life.

There was some discomfort. We slept under a mosquito net, but we still got bitten. The flies were annoying. You had to brush them away constantly. And watching them crawl on the babies' faces, the children's eyes, it gave you a queasy feeling. But did we have to get rid of all of them? I didn't mind them that much. I miss them, actually. It's too quiet now. The air is dead with their silence, here in the US.

When I was a child in Israel, one day the locusts came, arriving in a great big dark cloud. People caught them and roasted them in open fires. They were a delicacy. In Africa, people caught the flying termites when they swarmed, roasting them and selling them in little piles in the marketplace.

Here, nobody wants to eat insects. Now, nobody has any good thoughts about insects, except maybe butterflies, which are pretty to look at, and ladybugs, which kill other insects. The rest are evil. They cause millions of dollars' worth of damage to crops and expensive houses. They spread disease. I know; I've felt the icy cold chills and shakes of untreated malaria. These creatures are our enemies. In civilized places we've declared war and managed to get rid of most of them.

I don't have to brush the flies off my child's face. But still, I miss the insects. Do we have to kill them all?

Amsterdam

After leaving Uganda, I spent some time with my parents. Devastated by my brother's death and wanting a change, they had sold their franchise and moved back to Germany to work for the Dairy Queen Corporation, which was trying to establish DQ in Germany through their office in Offenbach. I felt sympathetic towards my parents, for my brother had been everything to them. They were less judgmental of me now, and even accepted my living with Steve. I went to live with him in Eschenau, a tiny Bavarian village where his band was based. It was a lovely, peaceful place, surrounded by fields and forests. Steve and I stayed with his friend Herman and his wife Susanne, in the attic of their house. Herman was a Dutch artist and herbalist, and I would often accompany him on his walks to gather summer herbs in the surrounding meadows and woods. The peaceful Bavarian countryside was an ideal setting for me to transition to being back in "Western civilization." However, there were increasing conflicts between Steve and the other band members, and when winter approached, Steve and I relocated to Amsterdam, Holland.

I spent three years in that lovely city. We had come there because Steve wanted to pursue his own career in music. We moved onto a houseboat, and I got a job, first at a macrobiotic restaurant, and then at an alternative crèche. Steve had been promised a solo album deal, but his manager let him down and it didn't come through. That wasn't the only disappointment, for Steve found out that his former bandmates, his childhood friends from Brooklyn, had cheated him of his fair share of the two albums they had cut together. Steve, to whom friendship meant everything, became very bitter. The open, generous Steve was gone. These last months since I had come back from Uganda had been very hard for him, and the problems were killing our relationship.

Although I loved working with the little kids, it made it harder to avoid facing the fact that Steve did not want to have a child with me, now or in the future. He had finally admitted it, after all those "wait until next year"s. I wanted to cut loose, and told him so. I no longer cared that he was having a rough time. I was getting tired of being weighed down with his needs while my own were being ignored. So I told him that this was it, and breathed a sigh of relief when he left for Ireland, where he had other friends.

One day a girl approached me. Her name was Mary Ann. She was American. She asked me if I was interested in being a partner in a bakery. Well, Wonderland, the crèche where I was working, was about to close, so sure, I was interested in something new. The bakery was Arbolito. It was owned by a Dutch baker and chocolate maker. He was getting old, and was limiting himself to only making chocolates for his candy shop, which was at another location. He was renting the bakery out, only using the back room for making chocolate confections once a week. Juan from Argentina had been renting it, had turned it into a health food bakery and given it the name Arbolito. Now Juan was too busy with his new restaurant and theater work to keep up the bakery. He had offered it to Mary Ann and she was looking for a partner. Sure, I thought, why not? I had had experience with macrobiotic cooking at Michael Losch's restaurant, where I had worked when we first moved to Amsterdam, and with vegetarian cooking at de Kosmos Restaurant, where I filled in when they needed someone. A health food bakery seemed like a nice project, especially since it was located in a quaint old street in the Jordaan, the old section of Amsterdam. When Mary Ann announced a month later that she was leaving for India, I found another partner, Wilma. She was a Dutch girl from Friesland in the north, still in her teens. We started baking, adapting traditional recipes we knew to ones which used only "healthy" ingredients like whole grain flours and a bit of honey instead of white flour and sugar. We made nut-butter sandwiches and soup and brewed tea and set up a few tables in front for people to have tea and snacks. We sold our various baked goods, as well as muesli and nut butters. We had fun running our little bakery, made just enough money to pay our rent, buy next month's supplies, and pay ourselves a meager little salary. We all gained weight. Wilma fell in love with a French boy. The baker continued to make chocolates in back once a week, and when we baked there, would advise us in all of our financial, baking, and romantic endeavors.

Besides working at Arbolito, I had a job at de Kosmos, a popular youth center in central Amsterdam which had yoga and tai chi classes as well as many other activities. I managed the craft studio there several evenings a week. A bunch of Stony Brook alumni had wound up working in the vegetarian restaurant downstairs. There was my ex-suitemate Ellen and her boyfriend Michael, now both cooks and expecting a baby. There was Jim, whose nickname had been Hamburger at school because of his favorite food, but who now ate no meat. Other ex-Stony Brookers were Jane and Dennis, who later married each other, and Bob and Paul. The person who had started this mass migration from Stony Brook, NY, to de Kosmos, Amsterdam, was Howie, the giver of nicknames at school and now manager of the restaurant. You could say he had a way of getting people to follow him. I had taken a longer, more circuitous route, via Africa and Germany, to de Kosmos, but still, there I was, working in the craft studio, occasionally helping out in the restaurant.

But Arbolito and de Kosmos weren't all of my life there, for Amsterdam is where I fell in love with dance.

It started out with a chance remark by Steve about my inherent clumsiness. I knew I was a klutz, just as I knew the time was ripe for us to split up for good. The role of constant emotional supporter had become an intolerable burden. When Steve left, it felt good to be free to pursue my own interests.

The first interest I pursued was Graziella Martinez's dance class. It was true that I was clumsy. I was one of those people who, all through junior high, high school, and college, never could dance. I was too scared to move. But I started to attend her classes, fascinated by her exotic moves. There were bits and hints of other worlds—Egyptian frescos, Aztec and Mayan art, Isadora Duncan, things remembered in a dream—but they were uniquely hers. She had a style I had never seen before and have not seen since, though many years later I saw breakdancers perform some of her moves on the street.

I attended all of Graziella's classes, never missing one. They were hard, for her style was not only aesthetic but also very athletic and acrobatic, but to my surprise I started improving. The months went by, then years, and gradually, imperceptibly, I realized that I had become a "dancer." Graziella choreographed and put together several shows during the three years I was in Amsterdam, and I saw every performance, charmed by her geometric movements, her dreamlike choreography. I sometimes watched her rehearse with her group, hoping she would notice my interest and ask me to join her troupe. I would approach her hesitatingly, trying to convey how much I liked her dance, and how much I would love to play any small part in the next show. "Just come to class, Noemi," she would say in her Argentine-accented halting English, and that would be the end of it.

The rest of my life, my evening job at the craft studio and my role as baker-partner at Arbolito, all took second place to my dance life. After a while Graziella's classes twice a week were not enough. I wanted to dance every day. I took some classes with Pauline de Groot, a former student of Martha Graham. I learned from her technique, but it seemed so dull and mundane compared to Graziella's magic. I tried to satisfy my need for dance by going dancing several nights a week at de Melkweg, a youth center which featured rock groups, but I wanted something else.

148

De Melkweg also featured all kinds of theater groups, which would often teach theater workshops in the days after the performance. I attended these classes, delighting in their fresh approaches to movement and interrelationships. One performer was a soloist named Mitsutaka Ishi. I found his show impenetrable but strangely beautiful. When I attended his workshop, I found he was as impenetrable as on the stage. Although he talked at great length about his dance and its meaning, I understood very little of it. It had something to do with not trying and a lot of abstract symbolism and imagery that sounded very lofty and idealistic, but I could not translate it for my body. He would say things like, "When you lift your arm, you must give birth to a universe under your armpit." Still, it was interesting, and was in the category of life I called dance. Ishi wound up staying in Amsterdam and holding a daily workshop in his studio, which was also where he lived.

Soon a regular group started attending his workshop. Besides Ishi and me, there were six others. There was Silvia, a blond German girl with whom I became close friends. Silvia also didn't understand what was going on, but she was a romantic, given to wearing flowing pink gowns and shawls, and she just liked the poetic sound of Ishi's words. Then there was Sidonie, a tall, very thin French girl given to collecting vintage clothes at the flea market and resewing them into her own unique creations. She eventually opened her own dress shop, and I wound up moving out of my houseboat, which was terribly damp in winter, and rooming in a house with her near the Vondelpark. Sidonie was an intellectual, and would endlessly discuss and analyze Ishi's dance over coffee, though I had the feeling that she too had little idea of what it was about. There was Gary, an American who owned a macrobiotic restaurant with his twin brother. Although he had no dance experience, Gary seemed to know what was going on, for he and Ishi had a special rapport between them, often laughing about some private joke together. Then there was the quiet

Japanese boy whose name I've forgotten. He worked in the restaurant of de Melkweg and spoke very little English. He would come sometimes, but seldom spoke. Finally there were Eiko and Koma. They were a young Japanese couple, completely and wholeheartedly devoted to dance. Their earnestness and seriousness were striking, even among dancers. Whether they understood Ishi or not didn't matter. They were there to dance, and mostly worked on their own dance. Nothing else concerned them.

The workshop sometimes lasted all day, and even all night, with us talking deep into the night. Ishi would cook us a dinner of tempura and rice, each of us eventually falling asleep on the spread-out mattresses, with Ishi going around and tucking everyone in with his blankets. In the morning he would be up and off to the fish market before the rest woke up, returning to cook us a breakfast of fried fish and rice.

So I was part of Ishi's group. Not that I asked to belong to it, not that I especially wanted to be there, and not that I felt any kinship with this kind of dance. But I was unquestionably accepted here. After some time Ishi's group started getting recognized. We put on some performances at de Melkweg, then at a museum. I enjoyed the excitement and status of being a performing dancer, yet felt a little absurd doing a show I didn't understand. For the dance still meant nothing to me. Ishi and Gary kept laughing. Maybe it was some private joke of theirs. It seemed to me, sometimes, that Ishi was just fooling everyone with his high-sounding arty words. As Ishi talked more about his life, some pieces of the dance started making more sense, but not the essence. He told about his failed love affair with an American girl, with whom he had wanted to have a child. So that was why he often came onto the stage carrying a baby carriage! Were we all just puppets in Ishi's private psychological fantasies? Was it all a sham, with no one telling that Ishi, the emperor, really had no clothes?

Why couldn't I be in Graziella's group, where I really

longed to be? I kept trying, attending every single one of her classes, attempting to speak to her, every year hoping I could finally be in her show, but to no avail. As much as I loved taking Graziella's dance classes, being in Ishi's troupe, and dancing many a night away at de Melkweg, I wasn't successful in doing the kind of dance I really wanted to do.

I also wanted a boyfriend, but had no luck there either. The spiritual types at de Kosmos bored me, and the more colorful, creative ones at de Melkweg whom I managed to hook up with were only interested in one-night stands. I got a crush on Miguel, the macrobiotic baker from Spain who sold his bread to Arbolito. I fantasized sizzling scenes of us going at it in the back of the bakery, but when we did have sex it was a disappointment, for he turned out to love heroin and not much else. I then took up with Victor, one of Graziella's actors from Argentina, but he was into this other girl so it didn't last long. Next, I got a hankering for Fernando, a sculptor also from Spain, but he didn't speak much English, and so it took me way too long to figure out that he was in love with Raoul, his roommate on their houseboat.

Sidonie talked of doing her own dance, and went to New York. I decided to go back to Berkeley. I missed the clear sunny days there. Wilma had married her French boyfriend and was expecting a baby, and we arranged for a Dutch couple to take over Arbolito. Silvia saw me off at the airport.

I visited Amsterdam several years later, and talked briefly with Graziella, who was still dancing there. I asked the people at de Melkweg about Ishi. No one had heard from him for a while, but the Japanese guy, who still worked in the restaurant, said that he had gone to Germany. There was no trace of Sidonie or Silvia. Some years later, back in Berkeley, I saw an advertisement in the newspaper for a performance by Eiko and Koma. I went to see it, and talked to Koma afterwards. He told me that they had their studio in New York, but toured every year and performed their dance here. Since then I have noticed their performances advertised many times over the years, and I'm glad that their dance has survived and flourished. The internet tells me that Ishi is well-known in Europe, and that his style is based on a Japanese performance art called Butoh.

Descent into Hell

It took me a while to realize that the Berkeley of 1976 was not as idyllic as it had been when I had left in 1970, and that the sixties vibe was gone. My old roommate Eve was no longer there. I rented a room in a big house with some other people and got a job in a vegetarian restaurant, but when I came home nights, I was unbearably lonely. I wrote my friends in Amsterdam, and their letters back were bright spots in my life. Silvia wrote that she wanted to come study dance in California, and I sent her information about some schools, but after a few months she traveled to Spain and, not having an address for her, I lost touch. Sidonie wrote me letters from New York, where she was working on a solo performance. She said she was coming to Berkeley, but then I didn't hear from her either. Wilma and her husband, Daniel, wrote me that they had a second baby and moved to Eindhoven, a smaller Dutch town, and after some months I stopped hearing from them as well. During that time I moved to Oakland. I had met a woman who offered me a room in her house in exchange for taking care of her developmentally disabled little girl. As my former roommates weren't concerned with either forwarding or keeping my mail, probably some letters from my friends got lost.

I felt not only lonely, but very stressed in the US, and missed the gentleness of Holland. Whereas previously I had always found it easy to go to a new place, now I felt that I just didn't fit in. I liked my landlady and her little girl, but I felt isolated in Oakland. The one thing that made me happy was my discovery of bellydance, and I took as many classes as I could find. Eventually I moved back to Berkeley, into a small cottage in back of a house belonging to one of my bellydance teachers, and did housecleaning to make money. I started seeing a guy named Charles.

One day, I discovered some money missing after he left. Unfortunately, I went to his place and confronted him. He hit me once before I ran out, but the damage was done. He had broken my rib. I didn't know it was broken. At first the x-ray technician said it was just a bruised rib, but when the sharp pain just below my heart didn't get better, I was sent for another one. It takes a while for the break to show, I was told, and this time they said it was broken. I couldn't dance, couldn't work. I couldn't stay at the place I rented from my teacher; it wasn't secure. Charles might come back. So I went to a women's shelter. Was that where my thinking started getting weird? It's hard to remember exactly when I started noticing that other people's conversations had something to do with me, with my thoughts, and that everything was connected. Maybe it wasn't just my rib that had snapped, or maybe it was the lack of privacy, all those people in the same room. I would wake to a few seconds of sanity, my own thoughts, but then the talk and thoughts of other people would intrude, and the rest of the day was chaos.

My thoughts connected weirdly. The counselor said, "You shouldn't let thoughts of what people think influence you," which I interpreted as, "If you're worried that people will think something, they will think it." So it seemed my thoughts were being read by other people, and I could sense this in overheard fragments of their conversations.

The shelter's staff got me a job at Jack in the Box. I think I lasted two days. "Too speedy," I said. I couldn't keep up with all the conversations I had to monitor for their connection to my life.

The women's shelter arranged for me to move to a halfway house. I had been to the place on the UC Berkeley campus where the drums were played, and saw Eddy, a guy I had met previously, drumming there. Later that day I saw him at the halfway house. He was the house director, counselor, and cocaine dealer. "The drums sent you here," Eddy said. This made perfect sense at the time.

I didn't take their drugs, neither the cocaine nor the medication the psychiatrist said I needed to take. I had thought that being in this supposedly safe place would lead me to feel more secure, but the opposite happened. I was scared and distrustful of the people there, with good reason. Some were dealers, others thieves, and my mandolin got stolen. It was confusing, not knowing whom to trust. I met a homeless woman there who claimed to have psychic powers. I was skeptical. She had a Magic Slate, the kids' toy on which you draw with a stylus and then erase by lifting up the film. "Draw me a horse's head," she demanded, thrusting it at me. I drew a horse's head. She glanced at it and declared, "You had a black Raggedy Ann doll when you were a baby." For the first time since infancy, I thought of my first doll, indeed a black rag doll, whose memory had long ago faded into that twilight place into which the distant past disappears. I remembered seeing a baby picture in my parents' photo album in Germany, showing the doll lying next to me. I couldn't explain how this woman knew of my doll. Maybe, indeed, there were connections only crazy people could see, and my own breakdown had allowed me some glimpses. I also started feeling things I hadn't been conscious of previously, such as anger. I felt angry at my parents, for I sensed that they had wronged me, but I didn't know how.

The staff got me on supplemental security income (SSI). I took the checks and bought plane tickets, to Hawaii and then Amsterdam. In Kauai, I overheard someone say, "too many good things," and thinking this meant my vitamins, left them there on a rock. I communed with the spirits of the place. On a beach, with another girl, I took some mescaline someone gave us. She said it was her first trip. We went for a swim. A rip tide gripped us just as the drug took effect. Fortunately, both the current and the pills were relatively mild, but I saw she was starting to panic. I knew I had to keep her calm, so kept talking to her in a normal voice to keep her swimming. We seemed to be swimming forever, for that's when time stopped, but we did make it back to shore eventually.

I went back to Berkeley and then flew to Amsterdam on a one-way ticket, not knowing how long I'd be gone. I was planning to go to Israel and work on a kibbutz. There, I thought, working outdoors on the land, I could regain my peace of mind.

In Amsterdam, I visited the people who had taken over Arbolito. The baker was still there, and told me Wilma had left her French husband and taken off with their two little kids to an unknown destination. Nobody knew where Silvia, Sidonie or my other friends were.

I went to visit my parents in Germany. They told me that Uma, my grandmother, who had died some years earlier, had left me several thousand dollars. I told them I didn't want to travel with the money, and that they should hold it for me until I needed it. I felt very uncomfortable with my parents, for they looked at any sign that I was unhappy or that my life wasn't going well as an opportunity to blame me for my errant ways.

I escaped to Greece, to an island where I had spent a happy visit seven years earlier. I then flew to Israel and visited my mother's brother, Siegmund, and his wife, Betty, near Tel Aviv. I also visited my father's sister, Herta, who still lived in Benyamina, though her husband Fritz had died some years earlier. It was nice seeing them again, but I was uncomfortable staying with them, and not only due to the lack of privacy. I found out later that my parents had asked them to report to them about me, as was their habit. Many years later, my cousin Raphael (Raffi) in Portland told me that my father had paid him $100 to spy on me when Raphael went to visit me.

I went to Kibbutz Gesher. It was beautiful there, in the Jordan River Valley, everything so green and deceptively peaceful-looking under a vast sky. Only there were many soldiers stationed there, and during meals in the enormous dining room, hundreds of machine guns were stashed under the tables, and the din of several thousand people was overwhelming. I couldn't stand it, and took my tray to eat my meals outdoors.

I picked grapefruits. I liked it, except for the white pesticide residue we would be covered with at the end of the day. It wasn't as bad as it was for the people who had to do the spraying. When I mentioned it, I was told only wimpy Americans minded it. After three months the grapefruit season was over and they put me in the pickle factory. I had to put something on the cans, labels or lids, I don't remember which. "Maher, maher," (faster, faster) yelled the boss. After three days I quit. I went to another kibbutz, where some friends I had met at Gesher had gone. But the administration wouldn't let me stay there. Somehow word had gotten round from the previous kibbutz that I had diabetes, and this eliminated me.

I wanted to go home to Berkeley, but first I wanted to take a month-long yoga intensive course at the Iyengar Institute in Pune, India, a relatively short flight from Israel. I wrote my parents to send me the money from my grandmother so I could buy my plane tickets to India and then Berkeley.

To my horror, they refused. They didn't want me to go to India to join a cult. I wrote them again, begging them not to leave me stranded in Israel, and explaining that Iyengar, whose style of yoga I'd been practicing for many years, was one of the most respected and well known yoga teachers in the world, and that this was not a cult but a way to keep healthy. They wrote that I should stay in Israel until the following year, when they would come there and we would "talk about it." If I needed money I should go to Uncle Siegmund.

So there I was, stuck in Israel, a place I was beginning to abhor, and dependent on my relatives. Being independent of my family's control had been a driving force in my life, but now I found myself at their mercy.

When I asked my uncle for money, he would give me 100

liras, about $10. Not enough to get me through the year. I went to Kibbutz Dorot, where my brother is buried. My parents had donated a large sum to have a playground constructed there in his memory. My mother's distant relation Zora lived at the kibbutz, and my parents stayed there on their regular trips to Israel. I asked Zora if I could work as a volunteer there. The answer was no, I could only have dinner and stay overnight. When morning came, she drove me to the bus station.

I hitched to Nueba, a beach on the Red Sea south of Eilat where a hippy enclave had sprung up, near a melon-packing warehouse which provided sporadic employment. I set up a tarp and camped there, but soon found it was not a nice society. These were not the flower children of the sixties, but a collection of misfits, some nice, some quite nasty. There was one guy, Baruch, who had a big tent and one night invited everyone on the beach for a feast. He sat down at the head of the party, playing sheik, then suddenly he pointed a finger at me. "You," he said, "get out of my tent."

I was stunned. "Why?" I asked.

"You didn't say hello to me earlier today," he said.

"I didn't see you earlier today," I said.

"Out," he shouted.

I had no desire to stay there, and left with the impression that he had just needed to humiliate someone and I happened to be an easy target, being a woman with no male protector.

One time I was walking along the beach when I saw an Israeli soldier walking in the dunes. "You!" he said, "Come here!"

"Why?" I asked.

"I have a tent near here. You come in my tent and drink coffee."

There was no way I was going into this guy's tent. I started walking away.

"Hey!" he yelled, pointing his gun at me. "You come with me or I shoot."

I kept walking.

I left Nueba.

I stayed at my aunt and uncle's place for a couple of days, but I was very uncomfortable, realizing that I was inconveniencing them in their small, crowded apartment, for my cousin was now back from his army reserve duties and also living there. I felt trapped and humiliated, having to rely on their charity. I would go into their bathroom and bite my arm to keep from screaming in frustration, and throw up the dinner that my Aunt Betty had made.

I started sleeping on the Tel Aviv beach, hiding behind rocks, trying to avoid the searchlights and army patrols that scoured the beach periodically. There were seedy people there too. One morning I was doing yoga on the beach when a man sat down next to me and started masturbating.

I needed to get a job, but first I needed a place to live, and there was a housing shortage. I heard of a hostel with inexpensive rooms for new immigrants, and decided to go that route. Applying for new immigrant status involved a lot of bureaucracy and took many days of traveling back and forth between various Jerusalem and Tel Aviv offices. Hitchhiking, or "tramping," as it is called in Israel, was very common, as soldiers were always going on leave and tramping rides home. One time, as I was hitchhiking from Tel Aviv to Jerusalem, a driver picked me up and took me most of the way, leaving me at a junction where he turned off. As soon as I got out of the car and he drove away, another screeched to a halt beside me. A red-faced Israeli jumped out. "Are you OK?" he gasped excitedly.

"Of course," I said, "why?"

"That car, didn't you see? He was an Arab, with Arabic license plates! I saw you get in the car in Tel Aviv, and was so worried I followed you. Didn't he try to do anything to you?"

"No," I said, "he was a nice person, and I'm fine."

The man couldn't believe it, however. "Israeli girls get

raped and killed by Arabs all the time," he insisted.

I walked away. His racist attitude was so typical of the Israelis I met. It reminded me of how my parents had assumed that the black utility man who had knocked on my neighbor's door was a rapist, and of the attitude of the whites in South Africa towards the indigenous Africans. I couldn't stand such bigotry, and knew that once I managed to get out of this country, I would never return.

While I waited for my new immigrant status and housing to be approved, I looked for work. I answered an ad seeking a waitress at a seaside restaurant, and was told to come early the next afternoon, a Friday. When I arrived I was told to wait for the owner. He arrived hours later, and told me that the job was already taken. It was now Friday evening, and the buses had stopped running, as they do every Shabat (Sabbath). The neighborhood was not one I felt comfortable hitchhiking in at night.

"Don't worry," the owner said, "you can stay overnight in the lifeguard's hut over there. It has a cot you can sleep on."

"What about the lifeguard?" I asked.

"Yossi doesn't sleep there," he said. "Don't worry, nobody will bother you."

I went to sleep in the shack. In the middle of the night the lifeguard came in and raped me. I was tired, and didn't put up much of a fight, hoping he'd just get it over with. "If you go to the police, or tell anyone," he said, "your family will never hear from you again. Your body will never be found." I had heard that this area was controlled by the Israeli mafia. I kept quiet.

I went back to sleeping on the beach in Tel Aviv, but the weather was getting colder and rainier. Sometimes I let some guy pick me up because I wanted to have a warm, dry place to sleep for the night. During the day I would walk around, feeling like garbage, and wondering if I would ever get out of the hole I was in.

When I finally received my new immigrant status, I was eligible for a room in the hostel, and moved in. There were people there from the US, the Soviet Union, Ethiopia and other places. My roommate was an American woman who had decided to become a super Israeli. She pretended not to understand English, and when she did speak a few words of it they were with a heavy Hebrew accent. The funny thing was that she spoke Hebrew atrociously, with an especially strong American accent. She had also become fanatically religious, and insisted that the lights and all electric appliances in our room stay off on the Sabbath, and even refused to let me turn on the water tap. "Lo kosher, lo kosher" (not kosher), she would yell every few minutes, driving me crazy.

I got a job in a ceramics factory, and looked forward to finally getting a paycheck. After more than a month went by and they didn't pay me, I heard that it was common practice for employers to get new immigrants to work for them and not pay them, since noncitizens didn't have the same recourse to legal protections that Israelis did. However, one of the hostel employees was kind and interceded on my behalf, and I did eventually get paid. By that time I had found a better job. I taught English classes at a hospital, to the doctors and nurses working there. I liked this job, for the hospital staff were very friendly. Since this was a white collar job among educated people, I thought I would be treated better by the agency that had set up the classes. Unfortunately, they also wouldn't pay me, and again the hostel staff had to go after them. At my last class there, I told the students that I was leaving because I hadn't been paid, and asked them to use their influence to change things in their country.

I decided to try a kibbutz again. I went to one in the north, near the town of Tiberias. They didn't find out about my diabetes and I was accepted as a volunteer. My job was to drive a tractor which sprayed herbicide along the rows of newly planted cotton plants. The lever which shut the flow was broken, so it could not be shut off. The fact that this chemical was constantly dripping into the ground made me uneasy, but when I mentioned this I was told it didn't matter. Nobody I met in Israel seemed to have any environmental concerns. Herbicides and pesticides were what had allowed Israel to make the desert bloom, and their use wasn't questioned.

Anyway, as I used to wear sandals, I got a splinter on my big toe from the tractor's wooden spraying platform. As I was working in the fields, with dirt everywhere, it got infected. I had run out of my diabetes pills, so the infection wouldn't heal. I couldn't go to the kibbutz doctor for more medicine, for my diabetes had to be kept secret here. Finally, I went to a doctor in town.

He looked at my toe and got out a syringe. "What are you going to do?" I asked.

"Lance it."

Before I realized it, he had jabbed the needle deep into my toe. The pain was so incredible I couldn't even catch my breath to scream, just uttered a low groan as the air escaped from my lungs. "Hurts, doesn't it?" the doctor smirked, then pushed me down onto the table and disappeared. He came back after what seemed like a very long time. He sat on the examining table and did something to my toe. I didn't know what, since I could neither see nor feel it, for he was blocking my view and my toe was numb. After a while he got up and left again, and I raised my head to look at my foot. I couldn't believe what I saw. A big chunk of it was gone. A piece including half the toenail had been cut off! I stared in horror. Just then the doctor came back with some bandages and wound up the toe. "There," he said, "you can go back to the kibbutz now."

I don't remember how I got back. I remember only what it felt like when the anesthetic started wearing off. I begged the other volunteers for drugs, and mercifully someone gave me a couple of pills which helped get me through the night. The next day I was transferred from the field work to a desk job. This was OK, except that this office was literally a mile from the dining room. I got a 45 minute break for lunch. It took me more than 45 minutes to hobble there and back on my crutches, so I had no time to eat. After a week I was transferred to the kitchen, where I washed dishes standing on one leg. I managed to get my diabetes pills from a kind pharmacist in town, who gave them to me without a prescription. During this period I perfected the habit of going into the kitchen at night, stuffing myself with food, and then putting a finger down my throat to make myself throw it all up so my blood sugars wouldn't have a chance to rise. I didn't know there was a name for this: bulimia. I just felt that I was the most disgusting creature on earth.

I found out that the Tiberias youth hostel was hiring janitorial staff, with room and board and a salary provided. Thinking that this would be better than the kibbutz, I took the job. There was nobody staying at the hostel at the time except the staff. It was Friday, and the managers told us that they were leaving for the weekend, locking the cleaning crew in, and they expected the place to be clean when they came back. This seemed strange, but as I had no desire to go out with my sore foot I was OK with it. I was the only non-Arab among the cleaners. They were very friendly, but as I was new they assigned me the novice's task of cleaning the toilets.

We were playing cards early one evening after work when suddenly a deafening blast shook the walls, followed by a lot of wailing sirens. We didn't know what it was and couldn't go outside to find out. Later, we heard on the radio that a bomb had gone off in the town square, which was one block away, killing a passing motorcyclist and injuring several people. It was a holiday, and festivities had been scheduled for that night in the square. The bomb was in a garbage can, and was supposed to go off when the place was full of people, but had accidentally detonated early. I was very glad to have been safely locked inside the hostel that evening.

After my foot had healed enough for me to walk on it, I got a job cooking at a vegetarian restaurant in town and paid for a bed in the hostel. This got me through until my parents came and finally gave me the money from my grandmother. I took a flight to Bombay, and from there a train to Pune. The train was packed, but the people were so gentle and polite that the trip was very relaxing. I remember a woman, shoeless and obviously very poor, offering me one of her plums. I stayed a month in Pune, taking Iyengar's yoga intensive course. The classes were very rigorous, but it was worth it, and just what I needed after my traumatic experiences in Israel. The month I spent in India healed me from the year and a half in Israel. It wasn't only the yoga that helped me. I found the people in India wonderfully calm and the atmosphere there very peaceful, a complete contrast to the anxious, paranoid people I had been surrounded by in Israel. I had developed bulimia in Israel from the stress and horrible things that I endured there, but in Pune, taking yoga classes in the morning and Indian mandolin lessons in the afternoon, surrounded by serene people, I found myself again. I knew I was basically OK, and in time would be able to recover completely.

I stayed at a student hostel during my month in India and met many Ugandans there who were studying at the university in Pune. Sadly, they filled me in on the hard times experienced in Uganda after I had left. Many people had died. I considered applying to the University of Pune also, to study botany and Indian herbs. Pune was such a nice place, but I decided to go back to Berkeley instead. After the insane nightmare that was Israel, I wanted to be back in the sanest place I had found in the world.

Creating Joy

The Number 9

*I*t was such a relief to be back in Berkeley. I found a room in a house, started bellydancing again, and got a job at UC Berkeley's entomology department, working with mosquitoes for an encephalitis study. After a couple of months, I found a nice studio apartment close to campus. I was 31, and for the first time in my life, had my own place.

I discovered that there were other women who were stuffing themselves and then throwing up. It was a relief to know that I wasn't the only one doing such a disgusting thing. I tried some self-help groups, but didn't feel they were for me. I found the Overeaters Anonymous belief in a higher power ridiculous. In the other group I tried, I felt the other members resented me for not being obese like they were. I decided to work on this problem on my own. With the help of relaxation tapes, yoga, and a stable environment, this problem gradually faded from my life. However, there were new problems.

One of my duties at work was to inject mice with anesthetic and put them on top of the mosquito cages, allowing the female mosquitoes to get the blood meal they needed to lay eggs. At that time the animal rights movement was not active yet, and the conditions the mice were kept in were awful. Each foot-square cage was only supposed to house 20 mice, but actually there were twice that many, and the crowded conditions led them to fight each other, especially the males. They were covered with bloody sores. Also, my boss only provided one disposable syringe each week for the dozens of mice, and giving the frightened, squirming, sore-covered mice shots with a blunt needle disgusted me. I had nightmares about mice, and felt sick. I decided it best for my health to quit this job. Two days after I stopped working I got a

167

high fever and chills. It got better, then came back worse than before. This went on for a couple of weeks, by which time I had cycles of fevers of 105 degrees and chills that shook me so hard I thought I was having convulsions. I thought I had contracted encephalitis in the lab, and went to the emergency room, but by the time I got there the chills had stopped, the fever abated, and they told me I had the flu. The second time, however, they figured out I had malaria, and I was given pills which cured me. I thought I might have gotten it from the mosquitoes in the lab, but the UC doctor said it had been lying dormant in my liver for the nine months since I had left India.

After I recovered, I was hired at a summer program for developmentally disabled children, and enjoyed this work. In the fall, I was offered a job taking care of three toddlers while their parents worked. My love of little kids hadn't diminished, and I was happy. In the evenings, I took computer programming classes at Vista Community College and also started dancing with a couple of bellydance troupes, which was fun. I even got a pet boa constrictor, named Secret, and performed with it. Everything was going along really well. All I needed was a lover.

I had first met Marc in Amsterdam, but hadn't been impressed then. He used to go to de Kosmos, the youth center where I worked, one of dozens of people I knew there. One day I had run into him in the Vondelpark on my way home. We wound up walking through the park together, and when we reached my place I invited him up for tea. I remember him sitting on the sofa across from me, not saying anything, just giving me a very suggestive look.

I maneuvered him out the door. The next time I saw him again was at de Kosmos. I was dancing by myself as I liked to do. He approached and started dancing next to me. I danced away from him. He didn't bother me again after that.

So now, several years later, after my dismal time in Israel and lovely time in India, I was back in Berkeley. My romantic luck was no better here than it had been in Amsterdam, for I fell for some guy who neglected to mention that he was already in a relationship. Then one day I was waiting at the checkout line at Eden Natural Foods on University Avenue when the guy behind me said "Long time no see," and I turned and saw it was Marc. He invited me to have tea with him at the cafe across the street, and I accepted. I had Red Zinger tea, he had hot chocolate. He asked me for my phone number and I gave it to him.

He called a few days later and asked me to go to a movie. I accepted. I needed someone to make me forget the liar I had just broken up with.

The movie was lousy and pretentious. Afterwards we sat on a bench waiting for the bus. He moved very close to me, pressing his thigh against mine. I thought this was silly, but didn't move away. When we got to his place, I put my arms around him and reached my face up to kiss him. He turned his head away. "Oh, great," I thought, "another guy who doesn't like to kiss, just like Steve."

But he really enjoyed sex, there was no doubt about that, and I got very little sleep that night. Not that I minded.

So we started seeing each other, and I fell for him, like I usually did when I slept more than a couple of times with a guy. I loved sex with him. The way he would pin my wrists down over my head really turned me on. We tried other things which I'd never dared before, and I loved everything he did. I wanted him to be my boyfriend, to care about me, but he didn't want commitment.

I had some dark hair growing above my upper lip, which I used to bleach. For Marc this wasn't good enough. He said he couldn't be serious about me because "You don't care about your personal appearance." He told me if I would shave off the mustache he might take me more seriously.

I didn't want to shave my face, afraid it would make the hair grow in thicker. Instead I had it removed by electrolysis.

He said it wasn't good enough, that I must shave.

I hated myself, a feminist, for loving such a shallow guy, a guy who wanted me to shave my face. Still, I couldn't stop. My heart, my mind, and my body were in constant battle.

"Dump him," said my mind.

"I want him," screamed my body.

"I love him," sighed my heart.

And then I got pregnant.

I had started getting interested in dreams around that time, and joined a dream group. One day I was recounting a recent dream. In it I was rushing to catch a train, which was stopped at a station. There was a big clock which showed that I had 9 minutes before it left. The train was between me and the station, and so I entered it intending to cross over to the office to buy my ticket. Only after I stepped aboard, the train started moving. "Stop the train," I yelled at the conductor. "It's not supposed to leave yet."

"Once it starts moving, it can't be stopped," said the conductor, and I woke up.

"What does the number 9 mean to you?" asked someone in the dream group. Right then I realized I was pregnant, even though my irregular periods meant I was late more often than not. I went for a test the next day, and it was confirmed. For the first time in my life, I was pregnant. I knew I wanted to have my baby.

Marc was away in LA, and when he came back I told him. For the first time, he kissed me. He covered my face with kisses. We made passionate love. The next day I started bleeding. The obstetrician said there was nothing to be done. I had the miscarriage at home a few days later after several hours of intense pain. The baby was about three inches long. I went to the hospital and they scraped the placenta out of me.

Some time after that, Marc disappeared. He didn't even tell me he was leaving, and I was devastated when I found out from his friends that he had moved to New York. He came back after a few months for a short time, and it was then that I learned that he was using hard drugs. I realized I would never be able to count on him, and that it was over between us.

A Long Walk

On a late afternoon in November, I was walking to Alta Bates. The hospital was just one and a half miles from my home, but it may as well have been at the opposite end of the universe. I was going to have a baby there, and when I came back, I would be a new person, a mother.

The day I had been preparing for all my life had finally arrived, and I was happy and excited, yet calm also, for I knew I was ready. The apartment was spotless, the freezer stocked with meals I had cooked and frozen. I had crocheted a layette of tiny baby clothes, ordered diaper service, bought a used crib and a rocking chair, as well as a camera. I had spent the months of pregnancy taking very good care of myself, swimming and doing yoga and tai chi, eating carefully and measuring my blood sugars with my new home meter. A friend even gave me massages in exchange for bellydance lessons. All my medical tests were perfect. I had known from the instant I got the pregnancy test result that I wanted to keep my baby, and this time, unlike the previous year when I had the miscarriage, I made it to my ninth month.

It was still two weeks before my due date. At that time doctors wanted all women with diabetes to undergo induced labor two weeks early. I had pleaded with my obstetrician to let me go to term, for the baby was healthy and, unlike most fetuses of diabetic mothers, not too large. However, he said that there were risks of complications in the last two weeks. Did I want to take a chance of losing my baby?

I agreed to be induced. I was to have my baby on the day before Thanksgiving. I was to check into the hospital a day earlier, for they would start at 6:00 AM. The obstetrician wanted to go home at 6:00 PM to start the holiday with his family. If I didn't have the baby by that time, he would do a Caesarean. My chances for having a natural birth were 15 percent, he said. I knew I mustn't have a Caesarean, for how could I take care of a baby by myself after major surgery? Therefore, I was carrying with me a large bottle filled with an herbal tea I had brewed. It contained a potent mixture of herbs which induce labor.

I was not supposed to eat or drink after midnight, so a few minutes before, I drank the tea and went to sleep, wanting to be rested for the day ahead. I had just fallen asleep when a nurse woke me up to remind me not to drink anything anymore. Annoyed, I had a hard time getting back to sleep.

At 6:00 AM I was wheeled into a small labor room and started on an IV of Pitocin, the synthetic labor hormone. "She's on the Pit," I heard a nurse say to another, which gave me an ominous idea of what was ahead. Nothing much happened for a few hours. The obstetrician came in at 9:00 AM, and asking how I was feeling, sat down on the edge of my bed. I started yelling, "Ow, ow."

"Is it that bad already?" he asked.

"No, you're sitting on my foot."

Although I was not in pain yet, I was becoming very sensitive. I had a labor coach with whom I had practiced for this event. I didn't think very highly of her, for she seemed too fond of playing me audiotapes of her screaming throughout her own labor. Still, I thought it would be useful to have someone around who knew what to do. She kept taking hold of my hand at just the place where the IV went in, and this was excruciating. I told her not to do that, but she kept forgetting, and finally I just told her to leave me alone. The person who did help immensely was Jehudit, my tai chi teacher, who had offered to be there for me. She did tai chi, and focusing on the slow movements seemed to relax the painful contractions.

I was dilating slowly. The long hours of the day seemed infinite as I very gradually, imperceptibly opened up to let my baby enter the world. The pain increased and for many hours was very intense, and I didn't think I could take it for much

173

longer. I was offered painkillers many times, but refused. I didn't want my baby sedated. The doctor came in a little after 5:00 PM and checked how far I was dilated. "How much longer?" I asked.

"Still a couple of hours."

I groaned, but not from pain, although I didn't see how I could take a couple of hours more of it. I just knew he wanted to go home, and a Caesarean was quick. Fortunately, an angel intervened. After he left, the nurse reached in and with a flick of her finger, did what would otherwise have taken two more hours.

"There," she said, "you're fully dilated. Now you can push."

So I pushed. I don't understand why in every single movie or TV show I've ever seen where a birth is depicted, the pushing part is shown as the painful part, with the woman screaming in agony. Actually, the pain was over at this point. I just felt relieved to finally be able to push the baby the last few inches of his journey. When the baby crowned, his head visible, the nurse told me to get up and walk to the delivery room.

"You're kidding," I said, but then realized she was serious. Very carefully I stood up and wobbled down the hall to the other room, feeling that any second the baby would slip out and crash head-first to the floor.

I made it over there, and the doctor told me to push very gently as he eased out the head, and then, crying robustly, out slid the rest. He was laid on my chest and I looked into the bright, intelligent eyes of my son, at his perfect face. It was 6:10 PM. "I didn't want you to get discouraged," the doctor told me later, "but your chances of avoiding a Caesarean were actually only 5 percent."

I'm a Mom

I had always wanted to be a mother, and now I slipped blissfully, if sometimes exhaustedly, into that role. I loved my baby so. He was so sweet. Some days were hard, like the time I had to take him to the emergency room when his face swelled up from an allergic reaction, and sometimes I was sad that I couldn't share all of his many milestones and achievements with a partner. Yet there was so much more joy to make up for any sorrow. He was so bright and active and curious. Every day was an adventure, every outing full of discoveries. One day, while I was at a playground watching Noah play in the sand, I noticed a strange feeling. It took me a while to realize that what I felt was contentment.

I had written my parents about my pregnancy after I was some months along and the ultrasound showed a healthy baby, assuring them that I would be able to take care of myself and the baby and would not need any financial help from them. I thought that news of a grandchild might bring some joy into their lives, for they had never gotten over my brother's death, but that was not their reaction. My father had only written me of the suffering both my child and I could expect because I was single, while my mother described her painful miscarriage and the torturous difficult deliveries, stillbirths and dead babies her sister-in-law Betty had endured. I hadn't let their negativity faze me, however, for I was too happy and confident that I was doing the right thing. I joined a single pregnant women's group, and their support was wonderful. After the birth, I let my parents know that it had gone flawlessly, that the baby was born perfectly healthy, and that we were both doing just fine.

They visited when Noah was a couple of months old. After trying in vain to find something wrong with him, they did love their grandson, for there was no denying he was wonderful. However, they were very disapproving of me, telling me that I

175

should be ashamed of accepting government aid. According to my mother, I was a "bad daughter" who brought shame to the family, while my father accused me of having done nothing with my life. When I replied that I was proud of having hitchhiked across Africa and of teaching there, of having studied dance for years with amazing teachers and of performing with them, and of my work with disabled kids, he seemed genuinely surprised that I found these things worthwhile. Ironically, while my father accused me of being immoral because I supported my child with government money, apparently he didn't think there was anything wrong with shirking his legal obligations to the government, for after he died I discovered that he owed a lot more money for years of unpaid taxes than I ever received in welfare. I, on the other hand, more than made it up to the government with my tax money in later years.

I gave up bellydancing, but knew that because of my diabetes, I had to work at staying healthy, especially now that I was taking insulin, the pills being contraindicated during pregnancy and breastfeeding. I couldn't go swimming now with a baby, so I went to a bookstore and copied down the exercises from the Jane Fonda Workout book. I did these religiously in the evenings when Noah was napping, and pretty soon had them memorized. I also continued to cook and eat healthily, my days of bulimia in Israel now just a distant memory. Later I bought a mini-trampoline, which Noah also loved to play on.

I stayed in touch with some of the mothers from the single pregnant women's group, and our babies played together. After a few months the other moms got jobs and put their babies in childcare. I didn't want to do that; I wanted to stay with my baby. I had a studio apartment where the rent was cheap, and I knew how to live well on a frugal budget. After all, I had lived in a mud hut in Africa, and knew happiness wasn't based on possessions. So I stayed on welfare and food stamps, did my shopping at garage sales, and found another playgroup for Noah with other stay-at-home moms and their babies. When he was two, I found a cooperative children's club, where I always stayed and helped.

I spent a lot of time outdoors with Noah, taking him to all the different playgrounds and parks in Berkeley, including Tilden Regional Park. Noah never tired of visiting the Little Farm there, as he especially loved animals. Our apartment was a half block from UC Berkeley, and the campus became our back yard. Noah learned to run and skip there, and play ball, and frisbee, and ride his tricycle, and throw pebbles in the stream, and feed the squirrels, and roll down the grassy hills. He got his first bee sting there, and learned the names of the different birds.

My parents came every year or two when my son was growing up, staying for at least a month each time. The visits were very stressful, for they continued to view me negatively. My father acted hurt and my mother lashed out at me if I objected to any of their demands. To my parents, my saying "no," was an act of aggression. If I expressed any of my needs, they told me I was being selfish for thinking of myself after they had come thousands of miles to see me. Once, when Noah was still a baby and my mother arrived with a bad cold, I asked her to wear a cloth face mask I had bought to protect him. She dismissed me as being ridiculous and refused. Noah then became sick and was very fussy. After spending a sleepless night with him, I asked them to relieve me for two hours so I could take a break and go swimming for stress relief. My mother told me that they had made plans to play bridge at the senior center and were unavailable that day. In vain, I explained that I really needed a break. "Noah is your child, and your responsibility," she replied coldly.

On one of their visits we went to the Japanese Tea Garden in San Francisco. As usual, my father insisted on paying for everything, but wanted to pay the least possible. At the ticket gate, he asked if there was a senior discount. On being told that it was only for San Francisco residents, he announced, "I'm a resident."

"What's your zip code?" asked the cashier.

Pretending to have forgotten it, my father turned to me. "What's our zip code?"

Caught with my guard down, I blindly fell back on the old instinct of obeying my father and blurted out a number. Since I wasn't familiar with San Francisco zip codes, it was the wrong answer. My father then paid the full fare as if nothing had happened, while I burned with the shame which had somehow been shifted onto me.

When my son was two, I found out he had gluten intolerance. I was very careful then to have no gluten products at home in order to minimize his exposure to that which was harmful to him. This situation made me think of the Dairy Queen, and I wondered why my parents hadn't considered my welfare then. I asked my mother if it hadn't occurred to her that it was a harmful environment for me to work in. She answered that they did not see my diabetes as a reason for me not to work at DQ, for it was my responsibility to refrain from eating ice cream.

I asked my parents if they would see a family counselor with me, but they accused me of suggesting this in order to "create problems." As difficult as their visits were for me, I put up with them because I wanted Noah to know his grandparents, for he was growing up in such a tiny family, and enjoyed being with them, and grew to love them. Things got better after a few years. When they saw that my son excelled in school and was very talented on the violin, my parents acknowledged that I was a good mother.

It was during one of their later visits that I observed that there was something wrong with my mother's thinking. I had been showing her my favorite earrings, a pair of little opal studs, which, as I told her, I had bought myself some years

178

earlier in Berkeley. "No," she said. "I gave them to you." I tried to tell her that this could not be true, for I clearly remembered buying them, but it was useless. I realized that she really believed that she had given them to me, and that my experience was irrelevant to her. I had previously noticed that she sometimes projected her own negative qualities and faults onto me, accusing me of doing the things that, in fact, she herself did. I had thought it was intentional. Now it dawned on me that my mother had a mental illness and could not help herself. I dreamt that night that my mother was drunk, although she didn't drink in waking life.

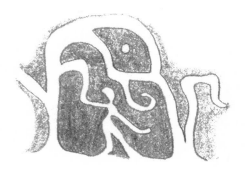

Three Little Pieces

Noah's early childhood years went by in a wonderful, creative blur. It was such a pleasure to see him explore the world and learn to master it. He loved our daily outings, from day trips to Lake Anza to overnight stays at the Montara Lighthouse Hostel. He excelled in all sports, from baseball, where he was his team's star, to iceskating, skiing and karate. He was awfully intelligent and so talented, and I was bursting with pride. I was too busy to write, but sporadically jotted some things in my journal. The following snippets are adapted from what I wrote when Noah was little.

The Crane

We'd been watching the construction on the Milvia/Center Street corner from the time they first dug up the ground for the foundation. Noah was fascinated from the beginning, always insisting that we stop at the "tucten," one of his first words. I'd never paid attention to such things, but now that my attention was drawn to it, I realized that it really was amazing. We watched the bulldozer and tractor and big trucks and cranes come and go, digging big holes in the ground, pouring cement, putting up big beams.

"They're like big blocks," I explained. "They're building a big house with the big blocks." He loved to watch the elevator go up and down as he sat in his stroller.

One week a big crane came and they started putting up huge slabs of concrete for the walls. We could see the crane, high above the other buildings, as soon as we stepped out of our apartment house. Noah always wanted to go "see cane."

One Thursday, as we were coming back from Provo Park, we stopped at the site and watched the crane lift some heavy machinery from the ground way up to the roof. It was an impressive sight, but it scared Noah. He wanted me to "care" (carry him), and pointing to the crane, said, "Mama, don't do that!" He wanted me to stop them, afraid things would tumble down like his blocks. Yet he was still fascinated and didn't want to leave. After a while I got impatient. It was time to go home and have lunch, I explained, putting him back in his stroller. He didn't want to go and put up a struggle. I said we could come back later. "No! Later, cane maybe gone."

But the crane wasn't gone later, and we went there almost every day for weeks, watching them as they hammered and put up the walls. We went over to talk to the men during their break. They offered to lift Noah up into the crane's seat, but he declined. He had gotten over his initial fear, but preferred keeping a safe distance from the big blocks and machines these large men were playing with.

Halloween

The first Halloween I dressed Noah up was when he was in nursery school. I bought two bags of feathers at the Rexall Drug store on Telegraph Avenue. One bag had little blue feathers. The other had big green ones. I taped feathers all over him, intending him to be a blue jay. "Oh, what a cute Indian," people remarked. So the next year, when he was in kindergarten, Noah was a Native American. I had carefully saved all the feathers. I taped the little ones all over his fringed suede vest, stuck the big ones into a beaded headband, applied some war paint and hung some beads and medicine bags around his neck. For the school parade, they paired him up with a cowboy. So the next year he wanted to be a cowboy. I bought the hat. He wore his vest, and boots, and mustache. "Don't I need guns?" he asked.

"No," I replied, but he stuck a water pistol into his pocket anyway.

The following year Noah was a swashbuckling pirate. He loved the sword. We made a hat out of black cardboard, and glued some gold braid on it, and a skull and crossbones. He wore a patch over one eye, and we went to a Halloween party, where he joined a dozen assorted ghouls, goblins, and monsters in a grand battle.

The next year he was a caped vampire, blood dripping from his fangs, his face a pale iridescent green. The following year he wanted to be a Star Trek character, but opted instead to be his own creation: a masked, black-clad crook. I was a witch.

Noah

When he's in a good mood, which is most of the time, he's a joy. If there's a possibility of fun to be had, a joke to be discovered, he'll find it, ferret it out and expose it. No pun, no play on words, can get by him without him latching on to it and using it to the fullest. He cannot go by something one can climb on without climbing it, something one can jump from without jumping from it. I guess if he has a motto it is: Squeeze the most fun out of life that you can.

But when he's in a bad mood, he's a different person. He's like a clam, shut in tight, and no coaxing can bring the little creature out. How to communicate, then, is a problem. He can't talk. I give him a paper and pencil. Sometimes that works, and he'll come out of his room and hand me the paper with what's bothering him written in a very shaky hand, so different from his usual bold strokes. Sometimes he can't do it, and I write down my guess of what the problem is in multiple choice form, with a little box next to each item, with the instruction: Check one or more. Eventually that works, and he'll come out of his room and hand me the paper, with the little uncertain checks.

The Old Apartment

"Mom, can we go see the old apartment?"

I knew he'd say that. There had been that extra-thick telltale silence just before he spoke. So I was ready, my voice carefully matter-of-fact: "Yes, let's go there."

We'd been shopping for his fourth grade school supplies in downtown Berkeley. It was so close, it was natural he would think of it. All we had to do was cross Shattuck Avenue and go halfway up the next block. I realized that it had been quite a while since we'd been there. The first few years, I'd made a point of going by the place, but now it had been almost a year since our last visit.

The noontime sun bounced up blinding from the asphalt as we came out of Kress's Variety Store. Shattuck was wide, with an island in the middle, and the traffic lights made us wait. It was hot and sticky, yet Noah waited patiently.

We climbed up Addison Street. There it was in the middle of the block, Heywood Apartments, the marble front entrance looking as elegant as ever. But the sign! The old sign that had been in front, it was gone!

"European Tailor, Ladies' and Gentlemen's Alterations," it had said, somewhat weather-beaten but with great dignity and a touch of old-world charm. Now there was a shiny new varnished sign, blaring the name of some arty knickknack store where Bella's tailor shop had been. So Bella must have finally retired! He had already been very old and ailing when we moved out, over six years ago. He used to call Noah "Mister," in his thick Hungarian accent, even when Noah was a tiny baby, and had given him a pop-up book once. I hated the pretentious new store, that tacky sign.

We entered the foyer and looked at the mailboxes. There was our old number, 22. The Chinese name on it looked as unfamiliar as ever, though it had been there several years. But the two boxes on either side still had the original names. Janet, the librarian and piano teacher, was still there in number 21, her boxes of red geraniums brightening up the windowsills in back. She and Neal had always been chatting in the hallways for hours, so that at first I had assumed there was something between them. And George, with his pipe, greasy hair, and ancient jacket, looking like he just stepped out of a Charles Dickens novel, was still on the other side, in 23. And Bob, who worked at KPFA, still lived in the same corner apartment. When I had first moved in, some twelve or so years ago, he had come over with a bottle of wine, for my "housewarming," he said. I could still picture how he had looked as he slouched on a pillow on the floor, for I hadn't any furniture, drinking wine, while I wondered if the reason he was grinning at me was that he knew that he was presenting, up the leg of his baggy, underwearless shorts, a total view of his crotch. How had I managed to get rid of him? I couldn't remember, just that I successfully avoided any more such friendly overtures after that.

"Who lives in Neal's apartment now, Mom?"

I automatically looked at the manager's mailbox. There was a new name on it. The last time it had been David, formerly a second floor resident who had moved into the manager's apartment with his cat.

"I don't know this person," I said, and then it hit me. He hadn't asked it! For the first time, he hadn't asked, "Where's Neal?"

I felt a tremendous relief. I didn't have to explain it any more! I had never figured out how to do that right.

"I don't know the person who lives in Neal's apartment now. It's someone who didn't live here before."

"Can we go up to our old apartment?"

"OK."

We went into the hall and up the steps. I noted with dismay that the place looked even worse than the last time we had been there. The walls were streaked and dirty, and the old paneling and wooden banisters were thick with dust. Neal had taken such pride in keeping everything spotless. The building had had an air of classic elegance in those days. That made up, somewhat, for the cockroaches we had to live with.

I saw that the owner had put in new carpeting in the halls. It was a hideous gray color, yet still couldn't hide the dirt and stains on it. The old carpet had been a rich red and gold pattern, and was narrower than the hall was wide, thus allowing several inches of the golden wood floor to show on either side. Neal had kept the wood polished and gleaming. And he was always vacuuming. That's what started Noah following him, as soon as he was able to crawl. At the first sound of the vacuum in the hall, Noah was at the door, "Nea, Nea!" begging to be let out to join him.

And so Neal had started babysitting for Noah, giving him a little rag so he could pretend to help with the cleaning, then letting him sort the colored pieces of cloth for his rag rugs. Neal was into crocheting rugs out of various colored scraps. His apartment was a rainbow of rugs, on the floor, on the walls.

Once, when Noah was two, Neal asked me to step inside his apartment. I was breathless, having just come back from taking Noah on his daily romp on campus, and I wasn't prepared for what he told me. I tried to argue against it. You couldn't really be sure, the doctors didn't really know that much about it, and the tests were not so definitive. At that time, all they could point to was an abnormal white blood cell count. It could be other things. But Neal kept pushing my logical denials aside until I finally realized that he didn't want my reassurances. What he wanted was for me to make a decision. I told him I needed to get more information, that I would let him know.

I left Neal and climbed up the stairs, thinking of another time I had to make a decision. It was at the Oakland Feminist

Women's Health Collective. My pregnancy test had just turned positive. Did I want an abortion, they asked. I said I needed to think about it a few minutes, although my heart was already racing with the joyous answer. But I had put all that out of my mind as I determined to think it through, to weigh all the alternatives and consequences. I had the answer for them in five minutes, feeling better for having gone through the motions of a rational decision.

So I called up some numbers and got the vague answers I had expected. It was probably safe, there had been no instances of children catching AIDS from their caretakers, but this was a new disease, there were many unknowns, and no guarantees.

I thought of the time I had taken my three-day old baby for his first outing. I bundled him up in the soft little baby bag I had crocheted for him during the long months of pregnancy, then went down the hall to the stairs. Just as I was about to take the first step down, a vivid image leaped into my mind. I saw myself going down the stairs, with my foot getting caught on some unseen tear in the carpet, tripping me. I saw myself losing hold of the baby, who fell out of my arms and crashed onto the floor, his delicate features smashed and bloodied, his piercing screams ringing in my ears.

I shuddered violently, clasping my baby tightly to me. For some seconds I stood at the top of the stairs, not daring to take a step. Then I recognized this vision as one of the many demons of motherhood that I was bound to encounter from now on. I could either let fear rule me, or move on. I walked slowly down the stairs.

So I told Neal it was OK with me for him to be with Noah. "Don't worry," he said, "I'll be careful." I knew he would be.

"You know Dan?" he asked. I nodded; I had seen his hefty friend at Neal's place a number of times. "I told him last night," Neal continued. "He just got up out of the chair, said goodbye, and left." Neal shook his head in disbelief. "When he got to the door, he got out his handkerchief for the doorknob.

He didn't want to touch it."

Well, things went on pretty much as before for another year, except that Neal got more tired than he used to. But he still kept on cleaning the place, vacuuming, dusting, polishing. One day, I woke up to the sounds of a crowd shouting outside my window. My apartment was right across from the UC administration building, where a crowd of students had gathered. "Divest, now!" they were chanting in unison, demanding that the university withdraw its investments in South Africa. I held Noah up to the window. "Look, it's a demonstration," I pointed out.

"Trayshun," he agreed. I got out some colored construction paper and cut out big backwards letters. I taped them to the window to spell out the word "divest," clearly visible to anyone outside. That was our art project for the day.

But Neal did not approve. "It's against the building rules for tenants to post notices on the property," he said. I told him I had been in South Africa and saw the evils of apartheid, and that issue was more important to me than the building rules. The demonstrations continued outside the window for the next few days. Then I got a letter in the mail. It was from the landlord. He had been informed by the manager that I was breaking the building's rule against the posting of notices. I was to remove the offending material immediately or quit the premises.

I was shocked and furious with Neal. "How could you do such a thing?" I demanded. "You didn't have to go out of your way to report me to the landlord. You didn't tell him about my boa constrictor when I broke the rule against keeping pets. Why are you trying to get me evicted now?"

"I was worried that he'd see it himself and blame me for letting you do that. Then I'd be the one to lose my place, and I don't know what I'd do if that happened to me now."

I wrote the landlord back that since the letters were on the inside of the window, they were technically in my apartment, where I had a right to put up anything I wanted. So the letters stayed on the windows for the duration of the demonstrations.

Then, when Noah was three and a half, we moved. The one-room studio was no longer big enough to contain a very active little boy and me, so I found a two-bedroom apartment a few blocks away. As I was packing, Noah kept getting in the way, so I asked Neal to take him to the YMCA's kindergym. Some hours later they returned, Neal carrying Noah, who had a bloody toe. Neal deposited him on the floor. "He got it banged in the door," he said.

"I'll take care of it," I said gratefully.

I cleaned the apartment for hours, for I wanted my deposit back. I thought I had done a good job, but when Neal came by to inspect it, he looked around disapprovingly. There was a big rust stain in the kitchen sink. I told him I had scrubbed it and soaked it and scrubbed it again, and that was the cleanest it would get. Still, Neal insisted on getting his own cleanser and scrubbing it another hour before admitting that it wouldn't come out.

We still visited with Neal for some months afterwards, but he gradually got weaker. The visits became less frequent. I did not know if it was because of his health, or if he was purposefully, gradually, weaning Noah away from him. Yet Noah kept asking for him. Neal came to Noah's fourth birthday party. "There," Neal said to me as he was leaving, "I think that'll satisfy him awhile." When he grew too ill to take care of the building, Neal moved in with his mother. I told Noah that Neal was sick, and he drew him a pretty card with flowers and a rainbow. We still kept in touch by phone.

I was taking an immunology class where I learned the details of Neal's disease, of the virus that kept changing its coat to avoid the immune system. "Hold on," I told him, not knowing what else to say. "They're working on a cure, just hold on."

"Yeah," he said, but he wasn't convinced, I knew, and

neither was I.

One day, about a year after we moved, I called his mother's house and asked to talk to him. She told me that Neal had died the night before. "He had just finished talking to his brother on the phone," she said. "I was reading, then I looked up from my book and he was gone. The doctors said his heart just gave out."

It took me several days to find the courage to tell Noah. When I finally did, I don't think he really understood that Neal was dead. It took quite a few visits to the old apartment to convince Noah that Neal was gone.

Lucid Dream

I was walking with my mother on Telegraph Avenue. We turned into a narrow doorway and entered a dark hall. "Have you seen the doctor yet?" asked my mother.

The "doctor" appeared, a very sleazy, dirty vagabond who began chasing me. I started running up some stairs to get away. I noticed some ivy hanging down from above. It looked so clearly focused and sharply detailed that it seemed surreal, and I realized I was in a dream.

I remembered what I had read about the benefits of confronting your fears in your dreams, and turned around and started walking down the stairs towards the man who had been chasing me. Knowing that it was very important to stay calm so as not to wake up, I held on to the banister in order to keep myself steady. I reached the bottom of the staircase, where the man was waiting for me.

"Who are you?" I said.

He just laughed at me. He had no intention of telling me anything.

This is my dream, I thought, and he has to do what I want. "Look," I said, "I'm going to count to three, and then you're going to tell me who you are." I started counting, "One . . ."

The man started attacking me, trying to force me to let go of the handrail so I'd wake up.

"Two . . ."

I fought back using tai chi with one hand, while keeping a desperate grip on the railing with the other. It was the most important thing in the world to know who he was, and I was afraid I'd wake up before I found out.

"Three! Now tell me who you are," I said.

Finally, I had him. I was dying to know the answer.

He looked straight at me, his eyes twinkling mischievously. He had a big grin on his face.

"You," he said.
The shock of the obvious woke me up.

From Welfare Mom to Molecular Biologist

When Noah was three I took him to a co-op nursery school, where I helped out some days and had some days off. Having time to myself again was nice. I took painting and ceramics classes, for I had always loved doing artwork. I also felt the need to use my intellect again, so I started reading a molecular genetics textbook and found I couldn't put it down. Learning about life at its most basic level, with all its details and interconnections, was fascinating. The more I read, the more I wanted to know, and so I signed up for some classes at UC Berkeley Extension. I decided to go back to science as a career. I had always been drawn to various creative arts, but now I wanted something more defined. In science, I thought, I wouldn't be subjected to the vagueness that I had experienced in dance and other art forms, where egos seemed to determine what was valid. Science promised a more objective truth.

By the time Noah started kindergarten, I had been accepted to a master's program in cell and molecular biology at San Francisco State University. I was awarded a fellowship for two years, and also a faculty scholarship, plus my social worker got me a scholarship for books, and together with my welfare payments these supported my son and me. Most people didn't know I was on welfare. I didn't look the part. Being white, I looked more like an aging hippy, and I sounded too educated. They assumed I was a middle class mom. Still, I knew I was a welfare mother, and being at the bottom of the social hierarchy was demeaning.

I had been on the waiting list for a government subsidized Section 8 apartment for a couple of years, and when my son was three and a half, we got the approval. Nancy, from my stay-at-home mother's group, and her husband, Paul, were the building managers and told me about the vacancy. I was very happy because it was a nice, two-bedroom place with a view of the bay and a balcony, and we'd be close to Nancy and her son Ben, who'd been Noah's main playmate ever since they were babies. Therefore, when Nancy announced a few months after we moved in that she and Paul were splitting up and she was moving back to southern California to live with her parents, I knew that their leaving would be very hard on my little son, especially since Neal, the other person he was close to, was already very ill with AIDS. Neal died a few months after Nancy's family moved out.

So this was a sad time of loss for Noah, and I think the tantrums he had at that time were a result of what he was feeling but could not express otherwise.

After Nancy and Paul left the building, some other people moved in who were dealing drugs and doing other illegal activities, and were very nasty neighbors. They harassed both Noah and me. They didn't like me because I complained about the noise and the garbage they threw out their windows. The woman in number 8 used to call me "Cracker," and her teenage daughter enjoyed screaming at Noah and terrifying him. They spread lies about him and me, saying he called other kids "Nigger." Even the ones who did not harass us directly, like Darlene in number 5 who was a couple of years older than Noah, and her mother, believed these lies. The woman in number 14 once chased me up the stairs and pushed her way into our apartment, threatening to beat me up. Another time she threatened to beat Noah up. The woman in number 6 would block my path to the stairs and refuse to let me pass, and had her boyfriend come up and threaten me. I went to court and got restraining orders against them.

I considered moving, but other Section 8 apartments were in even worse neighborhoods. I decided that I would move out another way. By improving my situation in life, I would leave these awful people behind for good. This was another motivation for getting my master's degree. I wanted to put as much distance between me and them as possible, and getting the cell and molecular degree gave me that psychological distance, if not the physical distance. I thought that after graduating I'd get a good paying job and move out, but it took me longer than I expected to find work. Fortunately each and every one of those harassing us got their just rewards and left. Under Section 8 housing regulations, if you're convicted of a crime, you're automatically evicted. This is what happened to them:

There was a police sting and the people in number 1 were busted for prostitution and dealing crack. They were evicted.

The people in number 6, who had been throwing garbage out their windows, were evicted.

The woman in number 8, who had started the rumors about us, got into an argument with the woman in number 14, and in the process had a stroke. She was very young, so I think drugs must have been a factor. I saw her being carried to an ambulance in a stretcher, and never saw either her or her mean daughter again, though I heard that she had been left partially paralyzed and unable to talk, and her daughter, the one who had been tormenting Noah, was living with relatives. I would be a big liar if I said I felt sorry for their misfortune.

The woman in number 14 got religious and after a few months of shrieking "Jesus!" every time she passed my door, finally moved out.

Darlene and her mom moved out. Several years later I ran into the mom. I didn't recognize her at first. She had been very pretty and always stylish, but now she looked like a wrinkled old bag lady. She told me that she was recovering from drug addiction.

So I wound up not having to move out, since all the people who had given me reason to leave were gone, and I got my master's degree in the process, and eventually a good job.

During all the times that the negative things were happening, there were two things that kept me feeling positive. One, as I said, was the thought of getting my degree and getting away from these nasty people. But the main reason was Noah. When I became dejected about my powerlessness to fight my environment, I just had to look at him and see the opposite of all that negativity. He was proof that, in spite of the fact that I was a poor welfare mom, I could raise a kid who was bright and intelligent and talented, who excelled in school and didn't get into trouble, who was so gifted on the violin, who collected caterpillars in jars and watched them pupate and released them when they emerged as butterflies, who was so full of life in spite of growing up with so few people supporting him. And this enabled me to keep going and finish my degree. Having such a great kid gave me so much hope, and that kept me going, and for that I will always be grateful to him.

Slime Soup

"Please, Mom, can we keep it? Can you buy it and take it home? Please!!"

You might think, from that remark, that we were in a pet shop, and the object of my son's infatuation was a cute little puppy. Or possibly we were in a toy store, and he had discovered some plaything he could not live without.

But we were in neither of these places. Oh, it's quite true that Noah had a tendency to fall in love with dogs, and considered certain toys essential to life, but there was something else about him; something most people would not guess a nine-year-old would give his affection to.

For instance, how many kids, on their "Things I'm Thankful For" list for their Thanksgiving school assignment, how many would write, along with such normal, lofty things as baseball and TV and water and air and video games and ice cream and freedom and friends; how many would print in big bold letters: "FERNICHER"?

Now I was to learn he had really meant it. We were in St. Vincent de Paul's thrift store on San Pablo Avenue. I'd stopped in to scout their selection of winter jackets, when I noticed that my son was no longer beside me. After thoroughly searching the store, I finally found him sitting in a lime-green plush velour overstuffed armchair. He had a blissful expression on his face, which changed to one of anxiety when he saw me approaching. It was then that he made his heart-wrenching plea, adding, "It's such a nice chair, Mom."

Noticing the large bald patches in the green velour, I stifled the panic rising up from the pit of my stomach. "Not to worry," I reassured myself. I was experienced in dealing with situations like this. I knew just how to handle it. "We'll see," I announced noncommittally. "First, I have to try it out."

He got up reluctantly, and I sat down. I felt myself sink

into an incredible softness. A marshmallow softness that went on and on endlessly it seemed, until it was suddenly stopped by a lumpy, bumpy hardness at the bottom. At the same time, a thick smell of mildew rose up to envelop me.

There was no way I was going to let this chair into our apartment. Love has its limits.

"This is not such a good chair," I announced. I pointed out the uncomfortable bumpy bottom, but then realized that someone weighing less than 70 pounds would never sink that far down, but would stay suspended in the softness.

"Let's look at the other chairs," I said briskly. After a quick perusal we both agreed that the other chairs were not worth considering. "They get new chairs in all the time," I said as I firmly maneuvered him out the door. "I'm sure that soon they'll get a much nicer chair, and then I'll buy it."

"But I want that chair!" he cried. But it was useless. My mind was made up.

When we got home I looked at our living room. "Maybe he's got a point," I thought to myself. "We could use a comfortable chair." The little sofa was comfortable enough, but usually when I wanted to sit there I would find Noah firmly entrenched in it, watching TV or reading, with several jackets, books, and toys there beside him and no room for me. The little folding foam futon was either being used as a fort or for piling stuff on. The orange swivel chair was only good for kids to spin around in. Lastly, there was the director's chair, but that was so fragile-looking that nobody, as far as I could remember, had ever actually sat in it. Certainly I wouldn't trust a flimsy little strip of cloth to hold me up.

Anyway, a week later I was on my way to Lucky Dog pet shop for some crickets for Noah's lizard, and found myself passing St. Vincent de Paul's again. I stepped inside. We needed some drinking glasses. I found some nice ones and then glanced at the chairs. "Lime-Green" was still there, along with the others. Then, at the very end of the aisle, I spied a new one, a huge monstrosity. I went closer. It sure was ugly. Was it a rocking chair? Wanting to find out, I sat in it. I don't know how to explain what happened next. I can tell you that I didn't get up for a long time. There was no need to. There was no longer any reason for rushing around as I had been doing. All I really wanted to do was sit in this big chair and rock. As it held me in its firm but gentle embrace, I felt at peace.

Much later, when I finally got up, I took another look at the chair, hoping it wasn't as hideous as my first impression had been. Unfortunately it was—no doubt about it—ugly. But it was oh, so comfortable. I gave it a careful inspection. It was in good condition. The muted green vinyl upholstery, although dirty, was not discolored or torn. It rocked smoothly and effortlessly. I saw it was a recliner and as it leaned back, a footrest sprang up from underneath. I looked beneath the seat and saw, among many cobwebs, some electrical wires. I realized it had been at one time a vibrating massage chair, but now the motor was gone. I went to the front of the store and paid the ten dollars for the chair and ten dollars to have it delivered the following Tuesday. I took a last look at the chair as I was leaving. It didn't look so bad from far away.

The next Tuesday my son was stuck home with a bad cold. I thought he might look forward to the coming of the chair as a distraction from his boredom and misery, but he was not enthusiastic. It was not the chair he had picked; it could never be as good. "But it's green," I said (green, the color of the Oakland A's, being his favorite color), "and it rocks, and you can make it tilt way back."

"Like at the dentist?" he asked, with a slight hint of interest.

The truck came. From the window, we watched two men unload the chair out of the truck. "Slime soup!" He groaned. "It's the color of slime soup!" That's his name for split pea soup.

I spent two hours on the balcony scrubbing the chair. I

removed all the dirt and cobwebs and dead insects and spider egg-sacks from underneath. When I was finished it looked brighter, but it was still the color of slime soup. After I had dragged it to the living room, my son spent five minutes trying it out, then abandoned it in disgust. Even its dentist chair feature failed to win him over. I didn't mind, for that meant I could have it all to myself. It was my chair now. I could sit in it, reading or writing, or just rocking my fantasies. My big, ugly, slime soup chair.

Postscript (2009)

Slime Soup served me well for many years. It was so comfortable that even though its vinyl started cracking as it aged, and my economic status went up, enabling me to afford something nicer-looking, I couldn't bear to part with it. However, the turning point came one summer when my son was pet-sitting a friend's albino corn snake while that family was away on vacation. The snake got away from my son when he was playing with it, and headed for the chair. We tried for hours to coax it out of its hiding place, to no avail. The snake wouldn't come out. In desperation, we finally slashed the side of the chair open so we could reach in to get him. To our dismay, he wasn't even there. We then found him inside the heater, nestled against the pilot light. I tried to repair the gash in the chair and ignore the damage, but it was useless. It was one thing for it to be ugly, and even cracked I could live with, but ugly and cracked and gashed was too much even for my usually tolerant housewifey instincts. I'm sad to admit it, but I became ashamed of my chair.

In hindsight, I realize I should have had it reupholstered, but I didn't. I got rid of it. I looked for a comfortable new chair everywhere. I tried dozens of stores, hundreds of chairs. Even the stores specializing in ergonomic chairs did not have a comfortable chair to fit someone of my small size. Whenever I pass a furniture store, large or small, I find myself heading inside to try their chairs, to no avail. I've never been able to find another chair as comfortable as Slime Soup.

A Tangled Web

The first thread:

During my time working at de Kosmos in Amsterdam, I was sometimes asked to substitute for one of the cooks of the center's vegetarian restaurant. My favorite person there was Hans, a sweet, baby-faced German chef who could chop vegetables with lightning speed.

"Chopping is an art," he told me. "You have to move your knife just so, quickly and smoothly and at the right angle. Otherwise you will hurt the vegetable, and a veggie that has suffered doesn't taste as good as a happy veggie."

"But how do you keep from cutting your fingers when you're chopping so fast?"

Hans showed me how he held a carrot with the fingertips curled inward so the knife couldn't get them.

The second thread:

When I came back to Berkeley from Amsterdam in 1976, I had been away in Africa and Europe for over six years. Things were not the same as when I had left, and a difficult, confused time awaited me. A lot of the things I had taken for granted, like my ability to get by in the world, turned out to be illusions. I could barely stumble around the shattered fragments of my former life, but there were advantages, too. What my world had lost in stability, it regained doubly in magic. It seemed that a lot of things I had been unaware of were happening all around me. There were strange connections between even the most unrelated incidents. This was such a new and unfamiliar experience for me that I did not know how to deal with it. I felt as if I was entangled in a strange web, and feared that it was a malevolent one.

201

The staff at the Women's Shelter gave out bus tokens for us to use on our way to our various appointments with counselors and social agencies. They were little round metal coins with "Alameda County Transit Authority" inscribed in them.

One evening I found myself in downtown Berkeley, having to make a phone call. I had no change, only a transit token. I shivered in my flowered poncho, wondering what to do, for the rapidly darkening street was totally deserted. Then I saw two young men crossing the street towards me, one of them carrying a violin case. "Excuse me," I approached them, "Do you have a dime for the phone?"

The taller one looked at me disdainfully as he hurried past. He obviously thought I was just another one of the many panhandlers in Berkeley. But the shorter one with the violin hesitated, then fished some coins out of his pocket with his free hand. "Hier," he said in a foreign accent.

I picked out a dime from his offered assortment. "Thank you," I said, and handed him the bus token. He looked surprised and perplexed; he apparently hadn't expected anything in return and was trying to make out what the strange coin was. "It's for the bus," I called out as his companion hurried him along. "You can use it on the bus." He nodded, and I felt relieved. I had sunk very low in the last months, but I had let them know that at least I was not a beggar. I made my phone call and forgot the incident.

The next day I happened to run into Jerry, an old friend of mine from Amsterdam whom I hadn't seen since I'd left Holland. Jerry was a commonsense kind of guy. I had welcomed his earthy friendship among the theatrical Amsterdam crowd, and now I was overjoyed to see him, a bit of solid reality in my present shaky one. We spent the afternoon walking around, reminiscing about our Amsterdam days and filling each other in on various mutual friends from that period. It felt so good to be with a friend that my present unhappy circumstances seemed remote. Towards evening, as we were walking along Telegraph Avenue, we saw a large crowd heading towards campus.

"Where's everyone going?" I asked someone.

"Jean-Luc Ponty is playing at Zellerbach," a passerby told us.

"I wish we could see him," I told Jerry, "but it's probably sold out, and even if it isn't, we don't have enough money."

"Let's just go over there anyway," said Jerry. "I have a knack for getting into concerts for free."

So we walked over to the concert hall. The last handful of people with tickets were filing in, for the show was about to start. We found out at the box office that there were indeed no more tickets available, and absolutely no way to get in. As we turned away dejectedly to leave, a young couple rushing out of the theater collided into us. "Sorry," the man murmured, and then, in an afterthought, he thrust two tickets at us. "Here, we can't stay; you can have our tickets." And they disappeared as I stood gaping at the two stubs in my hand.

We filed in and had just sat down when the curtain opened on the young man with the violin to whom I had traded the bus token. For the next couple of hours I was transported to another world of incredible and mysterious harmonies, a world where unrelated discordant notes constantly fell apart and yet somehow wove their way back to meet in beautiful and perfect patterns. It seemed he was playing just for me. Maybe, I thought, he's paying me back for the magic token I gave him.

The third thread:

A decade later I was a single mother of a fun-loving boy who had just reached that developmental age when kids painfully realize that their parents do not know everything, and to be on the safe side, assume that they probably don't know anything. For some kids this is a traumatic disillusionment, but fortunately for Noah, he had a great variety of TV heroes whom he could always count on for guidance. He did just fine taking his cues from them. Like many kids, Noah also decided, again to be on the safe side, that since his mother didn't know what she was doing he'd better start taking charge of his life. Thus, Noah decided to cook. He'd watched Yan Can Cook on TV, and he saw how Yan did it, chopping up vegetables at breakneck speed. This was how it was done, and this was how Noah decided to do it.

It was at this point that I became concerned for my son's fingertips. I happened to know how to chop quickly and safely, having learned the technique from an expert chef, but if I'd said to Noah, "Hans from Amsterdam taught me that you bend your finger joints and steady your knife on them, with your fingertips tucked safely out of harm's way," that would have carried as much weight as an ant's flea. So I summoned up the one person who was a cooking authority for Noah, and I told him that it was Yan who had told me that chopping secret.

"Where did you meet him?" Noah demanded.

"I saw him on BART. He was going to a TV shoot in San Francisco," I ad libbed. "I recognized him from his show and started talking to him. He was quite friendly, and when I asked him if he ever cut his fingers he told me his secret technique for cutting vegetables."

"Did you get his autograph?"

"No, he had to get off at the next stop and there wasn't time."

He was disappointed in me. It seems only his mom could be so dumb as to meet a celebrity and fail to get his autograph, but he did hold the knife correctly, the way Yan said to do it, and never cut himself during his intense but brief cooking phase. He soon learned that cooking was uncool, and went on to other interests. I also had many other things to think about.

The fourth thread:

Among Noah's next interests was music. He started playing violin when he was nine, and became really good at it. He started out playing classical but after a couple of years became interested in jazz violin. One day I told him the story of how I had met Jean-Luc Ponty.

"That sounds like what you told me about running into Yan Can Cook."

"What are you talking about?" I said, for I had completely forgotten the story I had told him.

"You know, that time you ran into Yan on BART. How many stars do you accidentally meet?"

"Oh," a thin thread started tickling my memory. "I just told you that so you wouldn't cut yourself."

"You mean you lied to me?"

"Well, yes, but I did it to keep you safe."

"You lied, and now you want me to believe this other story that's even more ridiculous!"

"But this one is true; it really did happen."

Of course I knew this sounded lame, and of course he didn't believe me, and whatever authority or credibility I still had with my preteen son vanished into a tangled web of suspicion that lasted for years.

The Dangers of Writing

When I received my master's degree in cell and molecular biology from San Francisco State University, I was elated, for this had been my goal for so long. I had completed my thesis project in a plant molecular biology lab at UC Berkeley. The subject was the role of a particular type of transposable genetic element in the developmental regulation of corn. I had been awarded several merit-based fellowships and a scholarship, and had glowing recommendations from my professors. Now, I was sure, my life would change. Not that it was a bad life, for I was extremely fortunate in having the most wonderful kid in the world, but I'd been on welfare for what seemed like ages, and I chafed under the humiliating grip of public assistance.

Having lived with very little as a child in Israel and in my travels in Africa, I knew how to live well on very little money, and since I hunted out every available scholarship for my son, he enjoyed all the various activities, sports, arts, music, and camps that other kids did. Nobody guessed that we weren't middle class. Nobody except me, that is. But now, finally, I was going to move up to a brilliant career. While I was job hunting, I decided to treat myself to a literature class and a journal writing class at Vista College. I especially loved the writing class. After three years of grad school and the very technical mindset of molecular biology, it was a joy to express myself on paper.

I applied to a lot of jobs. One UC job listing in particular seemed to be just right. It was at the Plant Gene Expression Center in Albany, which is associated with the UC plant biology department. I had attended some seminars there when I was working on my thesis. I had all the qualifications, applied, and got called for an interview.

Besides the principal investigator (PI), several other researchers in the lab interviewed me. I thought it all went well and was hopeful. A few days later the PI called me and informed me that the job had been offered to someone else, but the person had not yet accepted, that if they turned it down I might have another chance, and that I should call back the following week. When I called back the next week, she told me that person had turned the job down, and it had been offered to yet another applicant, who also had not yet accepted, but if they also turned it down I would have another chance. At this point I asked her for some feedback about why I was not offered the job. She told me that she was in favor of hiring me but that not everyone in the lab was in agreement. She said she could not be more specific, just that some people there didn't think I would fit in. I asked if my references had been OK, and she said they had been fine.

I called my former graduate advisor at SF State and asked him what to do in this situation. He was surprised that they hadn't hired me, for when the PI had called him for a reference, he was left with the definite impression that I would be given the job. He suggested that, if the job was still open, I offer to come in for a second interview to address any concerns they had about me.

I called the PI, and she told me that the second person had also turned down the position. I asked if I could come in for a second interview, and she said that she would bring it up with the others in the lab, and to call back in a few days. When I did call back, she told me that they had decided not to hire anyone just now, that the position was being withdrawn, but I could reapply when it was reposted after the Christmas break. In January, I saw that the job was listed again and reapplied. In February I called the PI and asked if I was under consideration and if they wanted me to come in for an interview. She said they had just given the position to someone else. Hiding my disappointment, I asked if she could give me any feedback to let me know what I could work on to improve my chances at other positions.

She said that there was nothing wrong with me or my qualifications. She said that if it was only up to her she would have given me the job, but one of the other people in the lab thought she would be uncomfortable working with me.

"Why?" I asked.

"She's from China and hasn't been here very long. In her culture it's not appropriate for a younger person to direct an older person. Since she's younger she felt she would be uncomfortable having you work under her direction."

I was dumbfounded. I couldn't believe that she was actually telling me that the reason I wasn't hired was because of my age.

"Isn't that illegal?" I asked. She gave a vague answer about needing everyone to be able to work together comfortably. I managed to quickly thank her and end the conversation.

I remembered the young Chinese researcher in the lab, and that there had been some awkwardness when she interviewed me. I had assumed it was because of her unfamiliarity with English, but now I realized my age had been the problem.

I was hurt and disappointed, but what could I do? The PI was a brilliant researcher, I knew, but obviously clueless, like some scientists, about life outside her narrow specialty. I knew age discrimination against someone over 40 was illegal, but she apparently didn't. This was the early 90s, and at that time this issue wasn't as widely publicized in the workplace as it became later.

I didn't think there was anything I could do about it. If I made a formal complaint, their legal department would quickly educate her and she'd deny everything. I decided to move on. But first I wanted to let the PI and the people in the lab who interviewed me know that what they did was wrong and unfair. I wrote them a brief, polite letter. I mailed the letter to the lab and put the whole business out of my mind.

A few days later I got another job. It was a temp position at a plant biotechnology company. The work involved doing plant tissue culture, transplanting clones of genetically altered tomatoes for the purpose of developing tomatoes with a longer shelf life. I was very good at it, and I also improved their computer system for tracking the clones.

After a while my thumbs and wrists started hurting from the repetitive work. "Don't complain about every little twinge," my boss told me. OSHA rules were not that well-known at the time either. I kept working until I developed severe tendinitis of both hands and was taken off work for three months. When the doctor released me to go back to work I found my job was terminated. Since it was a temp job, they had a right to do that.

I started applying for jobs again, mainly at Cal. During the next year I applied to over 40 positions at UC Berkeley. I got a few interviews, but nothing further. It was discouraging to say the least, but then I found out about a City of Berkeley employment agency that helped Berkeley residents find jobs in and around Berkeley. UC Berkeley was one of their main clients. Encouraged, I started handing in my applications to them. I was sure this would give me the boost I needed, for they kept track of each application and got feedback as it moved through the stages of the application process. One day I got a call from the head of the agency.

"I've just spoken to a professor about one of your applications, and she says you wrote her a threatening letter last year. She said you can never get a job there because of that."

"I wrote a letter all right," I said, "but it wasn't threatening at all."

"Bring it in," he said.

I rushed over with a copy of the letter, glad that I keep everything.

"Is this threatening?" I asked.

"No way," he said, making more copies. "I have a friend at

the UC Berkeley personnel office. I'm going to show this to her and see if she can find out more about what's going on. In the meantime, I think you should file a complaint with the Equal Employment Opportunity Commission (EEOC). It looks like you're being blackballed, and that's not right. You should start looking for a lawyer too."

I was completely stunned. That letter I'd written, I never thought it would come to this. I never imagined that anything I had to say could be seen as important enough for people to go to so much trouble to keep me out. I had never dealt with a lawyer. This was getting too surreal for me.

I thought of the professor who had let me do my master's research in his lab, even though I wasn't a Cal student, but from SF State. It had meant a lot of bureaucratic red tape for him to arrange for this. He had always been supportive, starting at the graduate genetics seminar he let me audit years ago. He knew my interest in plant molecular biology was sincere and that I was a good person who shouldn't be blacklisted. He was highly respected and influential in the plant molecular biology department. Surely he could help clear up this misunderstanding. I wrote him a detailed letter, telling him everything, and took it to his office. He wasn't in, so I left it on his desk. The next day I found a message on my answering machine.

"My advice to you," he said, "is to pack up your things and move somewhere else. You're never going to get a job here. Why are you still here?"

I played it over and over, not believing my ears. This was getting weirder and weirder. He was actually telling me to leave town. I called his office and finally reached him in person. "Everyone knows your name," he told me. "Nobody wants anything to do with you because they're all afraid you're going to sue. What you should do is get your lawyers together."

It seemed I had to sue them because they were all so afraid

of being sued that they had blacklisted me. Also, it seemed it wouldn't even be enough to get one lawyer, but would take a whole team of them.

I went to the EEOC, filed papers, and had an interview. Some weeks later I got a letter saying I had their approval to take this case to an attorney. I looked up employment lawyers in the yellow pages. The first few said they were too busy, but when I called up a law firm just two blocks from my home, they were interested. They consisted of two lawyers, a paralegal, and another person doing research. They agreed to work on a contingency basis, saying I had a good case. It was too late to sue for age discrimination, for the statute of limitations for that original job application had expired after a year. Instead, I would sue the UC Regents for retaliation for protesting discrimination, because the blacklisting was ongoing.

To make a long story short, this lawsuit took five years and a forest's worth of paper. Dozens of boxes of documents were generated about my 40-plus job applications to UC Berkeley, and about every conceivable aspect of my life. My journals were subpoenaed. The Regents had a high-profile team of many lawyers working on the case. My deposition took seven days. The trial took six weeks.

Their lawyers painted me as a greedy, lawsuit-happy psychopath whom nobody wanted to work with. The email trail detailing the blacklisting that the personnel employee discovered happened to mysteriously vanish in a computer malfunction at the UC personnel department. A number of other computer crashes at this office erased critical records of many of my applications where less qualified people had been hired.

Nevertheless, those two brave individuals, the head of the employment agency and the woman in the UC personnel department, told the truth on the witness stand, and the jury believed that I had been retaliated against and ruled in my favor. The Regents immediately appealed the verdict. At that point I decided to settle. I had accomplished what I had wanted to do, had taken them to account for what they did. They would think twice about blacklisting anyone again for writing a protest letter. Now I needed to get on with my life, for I had in the meantime managed to get a decent molecular biology position at a company doing research for vaccine development. I liked this job and didn't want to spend any more time and energy on the lawsuit. I can't disclose the terms of the settlement, but I was satisfied that I had made my point, and anyone interested can look up the case of Naomi Rosenthal vs. Regents of the University of California, at the Alameda County Superior Court in Oakland. I stopped writing for many years, however. Maybe it was because my job was taking up too much time, or maybe it just felt too damn dangerous to write.

Discovering

After surviving some years on low-level jobs as a lab tech, lab assistant, teaching yoga at the YMCA, and substitute teaching, I finally landed a job I could sink my teeth into. It was in the vaccines research department of Chiron, a company just three miles from my Berkeley apartment, still close enough for me to bike to work.

As usual, I started out as a temp. My boss used to sneak up behind me while I was concentrating on an especially delicate DNA task and suddenly clap his hands, trying to make me jump, but my hands were always steady. After some months I asked to be hired permanently but was told there was not enough money in the budget. Eventually, I convinced human resources that they would save money by hiring me permanently, since my benefits would cost them less than the cut to the temp agency, and I got hired as a permanent employee. Now I had such luxuries as medical benefits, a 401(k) plan, stock options, etc. After some years of climbing the hierarchy, I had the relatively good salary of a research specialist and finally felt middle class. I enjoyed doing the many molecular biology techniques such as designing and synthesizing long pieces of DNA or cloning fragments of viral genes and inducing mutations at specific points, and I became skilled at these tasks. I was content at my job, although this was not where I had expected to end up.

I had wanted to be in plant biology. While studying at SF State, I had worked for a while at a lab studying mouse DNA. I only took about 1/4 inch from the tips of the mice's tails for each sample, but with time, of course, their tails got shorter and shorter. I decided that a career in plant biology would solve my ethical dilemma, and took a number of courses that focused on plants. I found the classes fascinating. Unlike animals, plants can't move to flee from danger and can't vocalize. Instead, they have evolved their own sophisticated methods for defense and communication. I was interested in the genetic and developmental aspects of how plants manage their lives. I needed to find a researcher who would let me do my master's project in his lab, but nobody at SF State was studying plants at the molecular level.

Fortunately, the plant scientist at UC Berkeley whose course I had audited some years previously generously made room for me in his lab and allowed me to do my thesis research there. It involved transposable genetic elements, which greatly interested me, since Barbara McClintock, who had discovered them, was one of my heros. She had spent decades trying to convince the scientific establishment that their view of genetics as a static model of genes stuck on a chromosome needed to be updated. She had found evidence that there was a complex system of interactions between different parts of the genetic apparatus, with certain pieces, called transposable elements, moving around, turning genes off or on as they jumped in and out of them, sometimes even causing chromosomes to rearrange themselves in ways that hinted that they might be part of a plant's method for developmental self-regulation. Since science was conducted in a rather rigid patriarchal system partial to mechanistic, reductionist views, it took 30 years for her ideas of interrelationships to be accepted, despite the fact that she was a highly regarded scientist and member of the National Academy of Sciences, but she did eventually win the Nobel prize.

I did my research project on the regulation of one family of transposable elements in corn, and grew to love this subject. Working with these elements, known as transposons, was like being a detective looking at clues in a mystery. In some cases these clues were the spots in kernels of Indian corn, which told that the transposon had either jumped out of a gene coding for a pigment or been inactivated, allowing the gene to turn on and the color to be made. Molecular analysis of the gene's methylation status showed whether it was active or inactive. The size of the spot told me when in the kernel's development this event had happened, for the larger spots had allowed the color to be produced for a longer time than the smaller spots. Similarly, by looking at the stripes on variegated leaves, I could study the transposon activity in a photosynthetic gene. I researched the effect of growth temperature, sex of the contributing parent, and the effect of other genes on the activity of transposons in several genes in corn. It was also fun growing and harvesting the plants.

Some months after I finished my degree, I heard a plant researcher named Martha Crouch give a talk. She had found that certain substances and conditions helped plant embryos grow in culture. Although she had been doing basic research, which focuses on how a plant functions and not on the application of this knowledge, she learned that what she had discovered led others to develop ways of cloning identical plants in culture, and this technology, which was beyond the means of poor farmers, was being used by large corporations to grow plantations of identical oil palms. This caused pollution from pesticides and processing plants, destruction of rain forest, and displacement of indigenous people and their livelihood. She was so disturbed by what her work had set in motion that she quit doing research and was instead teaching and spreading the word to scientists to take into account the environmental, social, and economic effects of their research.

At this point, I started feeling uneasy about plant biology as a career, for it seemed that all the research was being co-opted and the discoveries misused by agribusiness. I was glad when I got a job at a children's hospital research lab studying intestinal development. Unfortunately, it involved dissecting rats while they were still alive, and I didn't have the stomach for that. I started applying to plant jobs again. I got nowhere with my many applications to UC Berkeley, but was glad when

I found a job at a plant biotech company in Oakland.

My son's swimming instructor happened to head the Berkeley office of the Union of Concerned Scientists. Some months after I started this job, I read in the UCS newsletter that the company I was working for had collaborated with a major tobacco company to develop a high nicotine cigarette. They had also been fined for releasing genetically modified organisms in violation of environmental regulations.

I was very relieved when I got the job in vaccines research, which seemed a less harmful field. Although prospective vaccines still had to be tested on animals, I didn't have to deal with this aspect personally. Since I worked on vaccines against major disease viruses such as hepatitis C, West Nile, SARS, etc., I hoped more good than harm would come from my work. After I had been there some years, an animal rights activist detonated a bomb at the entrance to the building I worked in, but fortunately nobody was hurt.

It turned out I got to work with my old friends, transposons, after all. I found one in a viral gene I was working with. I was very surprised, because it wasn't supposed to be there, but when I looked at the DNA sequence, there was no mistaking the terminal inverted repeats and the "footprint" of direct repeats of the target DNA. Checking its sequence, I realized it came from the bacterial culture used for cloning, and had apparently jumped from the bacterial DNA and inserted itself into the viral gene, which happened to contain this element's preferred target site sequence. I found it similarly inserted into genes of many organisms listed in the GenBank DNA database. Other researchers, not recognizing a transposable element, had assumed it was part of the organism they were sequencing and included it in their data. I contacted GenBank and informed them so that they could correct these sequences, and felt like I had done a drop of good in the world. I also installed a non-toxic alternative to the highly carcinogenic chemical used to stain DNA in the lab.

Eventually, Chiron hit some financial snags and was bought by Novartis, a much larger pharmaceutical corporation. As a result of the takeover, my department got moved to the East Coast, and all local vaccines research positions were eliminated. After over a dozen years there, I was laid off in August 2008, just after my father died.

Ima's Story

Ima, that's what I call my mother. It's the only Hebrew word I still use, except for Aba, father. Ima didn't say much about her history when I was growing up. It was only after my father died that she told me more.

My mother's parents were both born in 1888 in Galicia, which at the time was part of Austria. Her mother, Cäcilie (Cilly) Lipper, was born in Bohorodchany, a small shtetl near Kolomyia, now part of Ukraine, and her father, Israel Ring, was born in another shtetl, Pruchnik, now in Poland. Conditions for Jews in Galicia had deteriorated, so around 1900 Cilly's parents emigrated to Dusseldorf, Germany, with their three children. Other relatives soon followed. Several of the Pruchnik Ring family, including brothers Samuel and Israel, came a few years later. Israel and Cilly met and married in Dusseldorf in 1912. Because their parents had been married by a rabbi only and hadn't paid the high marriage taxes imposed on Jews in Galicia, these marriages were considered invalid in Germany. Thus Israel Ring was assigned his mother's maiden name as surname, while Cilly's maiden name was listed as Klapper, her mother's maiden name. Israel and Cilly bought a shoe store in nearby Remscheid, a small industrial town where many of the relatives had moved. A son, Siegmund, was born in 1913. During WWI, Israel served as a telegraph operator in the Austrian army. Gerda, my mother, was born in 1917. She grew up within a large extended family.

When Gerda reached adolescence, the Nazi presence started establishing itself in Germany. Remscheid, however, was a tolerant community, where Christians and the small Jewish community of about 300 were used to living and working together harmoniously. Her parents were involved with community groups, many of their friends were working-class socialists or communists, and there were meetings and discussion groups at their house in the evenings. Her parents, like many others, felt that the Nazis were a temporary fad and would soon pass. When Hitler grabbed power in January 1933, they did not take the threat seriously, saying that there had been other regimes in Germany that had come and gone.

On April 1, 1933, there was an announcement at Gerda's school that many Jewish businessmen had been arrested and put in jail. Frightened, Gerda started crying. "Don't worry," her girlfriends reassured her. "It's only the Jews who swindle people they're arresting, not the good ones like your family." Gerda wondered which of the Jewish people she knew were the swindlers.

Zionist recruiters started coming to Remscheid and giving propaganda talks to convince Jews to emigrate to Palestine. Gerda considered leaving Germany, but she wanted to go to England. Her landlord's daughter had found a job as an au pair in London, and Gerda also applied and was contacted by a family in London, but a British visa was too expensive.

Gerda wanted to learn a profession which she could use to support herself if she left Germany. She excelled in languages, and had wanted to become a foreign correspondent. An academic degree would take three years to complete, however, and she felt she didn't have that much time. Her father then heard about a new trade school that was opening nearby, where she could learn secretarial skills and get a diploma in one year. Gerda went to talk to the director. He was very nice, and assured her that she would be treated well at his school. She enrolled, but shortly after she started, the director suddenly vanished. His replacement was a Nazi, many of the teachers started coming to school with Nazi salutes, and the boys wore Hitler Youth uniforms. Even the math teacher kept quoting Hitler. Gerda dropped out then. Later, she learned that the director who had been friendly toward her had been transferred to a small, out-of-the-way country school.

Gerda had been close friends with the landlord's son, Karl,

since they'd been toddlers. One day, when she greeted him as they passed each other on the stairs, he looked right past her. She found out that he had enrolled in the Hitler Youth. Around that time, the man who had always prepared the window displays at her parents' store announced that he could no longer work for Jews, and left abruptly. However, his young apprentice, named Hermann Schlipphacke, said he would not abandon the family and stayed to help. Seeing that the boy had talent, Gerda's father raised funds for him to go to a design academy, and in later years Hermann became a successful designer and painter. After the war, my parents got in touch with him and they became friends. One of his paintings still hangs in my mother's living room.

In July 1935, after some weeks of training, 18-year-old Gerda left Germany with the Youth Aliyah, an American organization that helped Jewish youth leave Germany to emigrate to Palestine. Gerda was told she would be able to continue her education there, which she very much wanted to do. She and another girl from Remscheid took the train to Trieste, Italy, from where the Aliyah group of about a dozen girls took a boat to Palestine.

When the ship docked in Jaffa, Gerda was horrified to see a horde of Arabs storm the ship and rush on deck, yelling and grabbing all the baggage. She was sure they were robbers and that she and the other passengers would be murdered, only to find out that these were the porters who were hoping to earn a coin by carrying their luggage. Then Henrietta Szold, the American leader of the Youth Aliyah, came and put the girls on a bus to Jerusalem.

Hot and tired from the long trip, Gerda arrived at the Beit Zirot hostel in time for dinner. She saw a bowl of beautiful black cherries on the table. This cheered her up, for she loved cherries. She eagerly reached for one and popped it in her mouth. It was an awful, salty olive! No more cherries, just olives and greasy eggplant. And the only meat, when there was meat, was mutton. It came from the marketplace, where it hung in big slabs out in the hot sun, covered with flies, black with flies. The smell of mutton or lamb still makes my mother nauseous, and even after all these years she won't eat it. These first impressions of Palestine never quite left Gerda. To her, it was an uncivilized, hot, mosquito-fly-cockroach-ridden place.

Conditions at the hostel where she was staying were hard. Not only food, but also water was scarce, for at the time Jerusalem didn't have a municipal water supply with running water. They caught rainwater on the roof and had to ration it carefully. Many of the girls were just fifteen years old and away from their families for the first time, not knowing if they would ever see them again. Some became depressed. One girl jumped from the roof of the multistory hostel. She didn't survive. The other girls were given sedatives afterwards.

The promised educational opportunities did not materialize, for the Youth Aliyah was just getting started there, so Gerda only learned cooking and housekeeping. They did have Hebrew lessons, however. In order to help them learn to speak it, some local girls were recruited to live with them. This didn't have the desired result, however, for after a few weeks, these girls stopped speaking Hebrew and spoke only German, having picked it up from their new friends.

The area where the hostel was located came under sniper fire. The indigenous Palestinian Arabs were trying to stop the takeover of their homes by the many Jewish refugees. A Jewish militia group, the Haganah, was fighting the Arab uprising. My mother said that the British mandate made it illegal for the men to carry weapons, and they would have been jailed if guns were found on them. Since women weren't searched, when a Haganah soldier went on night patrol he would ask one of the girls from the hostel, sometimes Gerda, to accompany him and carry his pistol in her bra. This went on until the organization that sponsored the hostel learned what was going on and stopped the girls from such activities.

Around this time Gerda met my future father, Alfred Rosenthal. She didn't like him that much, but he, apparently, was crazy about her and wanted to marry her. She wrote about it to her parents. They were against the marriage. Not only was he a German Jew, which they, originally from Galicia, considered inferior, but he was uneducated and unskilled. Gerda had her own misgivings about marrying Alfred, and she didn't want to stay in the harsh Palestine environment.

After her two years at the Youth Aliyah were up, Gerda found that the only jobs she could get were either as a maid or doing childcare, neither of which appealed to her. However, she had been writing to a girl in New Jersey, and this pen-pal's father had offered to sponsor her to emigrate to the US to live with them and continue her education there. In 1937 Gerda made the trip back to Germany to see her parents again and wait for her US entry papers. She stayed with her parents in Remscheid for almost a year, waiting for the necessary documents, but as her sponsor was not a relative, this proved especially difficult to arrange. Meanwhile, Alfred wrote her impatient letters from Palestine which she did not reciprocate, and he got angry. While she waited for the papers from the US to arrive, her one-year leave from Palestine was running out. She had to be back in Palestine by the specified date or she would be refused entry, and if the visa for America was also denied, she would be stranded in Germany. She waited as long as she possibly could, but as the US papers still hadn't come in June of 1938, her parents put her on the train for Italy again, from where she would again take the boat to Palestine. She told of the last view she had of her father's face as she looked out the train window. "It was ashen white. Maybe he sensed that we wouldn't see each other again."

Since this time Gerda would be traveling by herself, her parents had put her in a compartment with two nuns they happened to see sitting there, thinking they would be safe company. At the next station, one of the nuns got out and was

222

gone for a while. Shortly after she returned, two Nazi officers came to the compartment and told Gerda to come with them. They took her inside the station and searched all her luggage carefully while a female officer did a strip search. They found nothing, of course. Just as she finished putting her clothes back on, the train started to leave the station. Seeing her last chance of escape from Germany slipping away, Gerda started crying hysterically. "Oh, so go then," one of the Nazi officers said in disgust. Gerda desperately ran after the train, screaming and yelling so loudly that the flagman signaled it to stop. Gerda threw herself inside, and the guard hurled her luggage in after her. When she had stopped shaking enough to make her way back to her compartment, the two nuns exchanged a stunned look. Gerda was sure it was they who had denounced her. Only when she looked out the train window and saw that the road signs were all in Italian, and knew she was safely out of Germany, could she finally relax.

After Alfred's demanding and annoying letters, Gerda intended not to have anything to do with him when she returned, but when her ship docked in Palestine, he was waiting there to meet her. "He looked so happy to see me," Gerda said. "He was standing there, beaming, with the biggest smile on his face, and all our arguments were forgotten."

There were letters from her parents for some time. Her brother fled to Denmark on October 4, 1938. On October 28 her father, along with thousands of other Polish-born Jews, was deported to Zbaszyn, Poland. Since Poland didn't let them in, they were stranded at the border. Then, on November 9 came Kristallnacht, the "night of broken glass." That night the windows of their shop were smashed and the store, like all Jewish-owned businesses, was wrecked, with the shoes thrown into the street. My mother learned that her father was allowed to return briefly in order to arrange the payment to the landlord for the damage done to the shop, for which they were responsible, and to liquidate his business. In December her father was again deported to the Polish border. The next year Cilly and most of the remaining Polish-born Jews in Remscheid were also deported. Her parents managed to make their way to Kolomyia, where Cilly had a female cousin who was a doctor. They were able to send only very brief notes through the Red Cross. They didn't write about their living conditions, but Gerda guessed from other things they wrote. "If the Nazis take over Egypt," her father wrote, "run for your lives. Don't bother about your possessions, just run." They finally gave their blessing for the marriage. When Gerda wrote in 1940 that she had wed, her father wrote back that they had celebrated with a bottle of mineral water.

The last note Gerda received from her father was sent from Kolomyia on February 11, 1941. Gerda still had some hope of reuniting when the war was over. When it did finally end, among the stories of mass carnage pouring in was a small trickle of miracles. Her younger cousin Siegi had managed to survive five and a half years in various concentration camps. Her parents had not been so fortunate. Thousands of Jews who managed to survive months of starvation in Kolomyia were marched to the nearby woods, forced to dig their own graves, and then shot. The rest were packed into cattle cars and sent to be gassed in the Belzec death camp. I hope it was some comfort to my mother to have a little son then, when she found out that her parents had not survived the Kolomyia massacres.

Aba's Story

My father, Alfred Rosenthal, was born in 1913 in Hamburg, Germany. His father, Hugo, a bank official, died in the first months of WWI. He had been serving in the German army on the Eastern Front, was wounded and captured by the Russians. He died from an infected amputated leg in Grodno, now in Belarus. Hugo's widow, my grandmother Lina, was left with two children, a six-year-old girl, Herta, and eleven-month-old Alfred. Their villa in Hamburg was sold and the money invested in war bonds. Lina then moved with her children to Frankfurt, where her mother and sisters lived. After the war ended, these bonds were worthless, and Lina had only her war-widow's pension to support them. After my father died, I learned that since his mother was poor, Alfred received a scholarship from the Orthodox synagogue in Frankfurt to attend their school. He was a scholarship student there for all nine years of his education, while his sister went to a more affordable Christian school.

When he was sixteen, Alfred stopped his schooling and started working as an apprentice for a wholesale lace import company to help support his mother. He found his job very tedious, however, with a difficult boss who complained if he was a minute late. When the Nazis first appeared, Alfred, like many German Jews, didn't take them seriously. In early 1933 he even attended a Purim costume party dressed as a Nazi, wearing brown shirt and pants and a swastika pin he borrowed from a coworker. This coworker was in the SS, but was always very friendly towards him. "If you're ever in trouble, you can mention my name and nothing will happen to you," he told Alfred. My father said he was glad he never had to rely on this promise.

Alfred had always been patriotic and proud that his father had given his life for his country, and now he was angry that as a Jew he was no longer considered a true German. As Hitler's influence progressed, Alfred wanted to get away from both the Nazis and his hateful job. His older sister had gone to Palestine already in early 1933 and started a laundry business there, writing that her mother and brother should come too. On November 29, 1933, Alfred's 20th birthday, he and his mother boarded a ship in Trieste, Italy, for Palestine. Since his mother had a source of income, her widow's pension, she was allowed to live in Palestine. Alfred, however, not having a trade or education, could only get a three-month tourist visa and for years was in danger of being deported if discovered by the British authorities.

Alfred was first hired as an errand boy and then went through a number of jobs in Palestine and Israel, but there were scant opportunities for him in the meager economy there. He also had a number of jobs in the US which did not work out or which he did not like, and that is the reason we kept moving. My mother, on the other hand, liked her jobs, first at the bookstore in Portland and then the bank in Manhattan, but she quit these to accommodate my father.

My father finally achieved success with the Dairy Queen franchise, and was very proud of his store. My parents could then afford to go on cruises during the winters when the store was closed, and this intermittent luxury was some compensation to my mother for giving up her career. After my brother's death, my parents were too disheartened to go on with the hard work their business required. They sold it and took an offer from the Dairy Queen company to work for them in Germany, and moved there. As Dairy Queen was unsuccessful in Germany, this job ended after three years, and my father went on to work for the Jewish National Fund, raising donations for Israel.

After my parents moved back to Germany, they took frequent trips to many parts of the world. I was glad that after their extensive travels, my father relaxed some of his narrow views of other ethnic groups, but he remained convinced that Arabs were an inferior and less humane people. He also believed Israel could do no wrong, and that Palestinians and other Arabs were solely to blame for all the troubles in the Middle East. He considered me a traitor for criticizing the Israeli government and sympathizing with the Palestinian struggle for rights and independence, and couldn't understand that my support for justice in the region didn't mean that I condoned violence or Islamic fundamentalism. Seeing that my parents could not change, and because I wanted their old age to be untroubled, I stopped discussing these issues with them years ago.

My father also had a tendency towards denial and making up his own reality contrary to facts, and this was what prevented me from ever getting close to him. In the last years, I had avoided, in deference to his age, mentioning any topics on which we disagreed. However, when he was diagnosed with bladder cancer and I realized his time was limited, I made a last ditch effort to reach him on an honest level about a personal issue that was very important to me. He often alluded to how immature I had been in the past, when we had not gotten along, and how glad he was that I was finally older and wiser. To him, whatever conflicts we had had were due to my immaturity. I wanted him to see that this was not the case, that I had very good reasons to act the way I did. I wanted so much for my father to understand me, and knowing this was the last chance for that to happen, I made my final appeal to him.

The main event that had started the rift between my parents and me had been their insistence that I work at the Dairy Queen, the family business. The fact that I had left was what had branded me as selfish and disloyal. I couldn't understand why my parents had never taken into account that an ice cream parlor was not a healthy place for a teenager with diabetes to work.

I felt that this was my last chance to get my father to really understand and realize that I hadn't been the selfish girl he thought I was. Maybe it was naive of me, but I thought it would make him happier to know that his daughter had been a good person all along. However, when I asked my father about it, he got angry that I brought up the issue, saying one should let bygones be bygones. Hadn't he forgiven me for running away? He couldn't understand why I didn't just forget it.

Now that time was running out, I wanted a real resolution, not more evasions, and tried to explain that I just wanted a better understanding between us. He finally emailed: The Dairy Queen wasn't so bad for me, he insisted, for afterwards I had gone and worked at Baskin Robbins in Manhattan.

I was flabbergasted, for I had never worked at Baskin Robbins or even thought of working there. I wrote this back to him, but he insisted that both he and my mother remembered me applying there. In vain I told him this did not happen, that I had worked at a cafe in Boston the first summer I had refused to work at the Dairy Queen, and the next summer, when I did live in Manhattan, I had worked first at a jewelry factory and then for a stock market publication, and never had anything to do with Baskin Robbins or any other ice cream store besides the Dairy Queen. I even asked my old friend Steve, with whom I had lived at that time, whether I could have forgotten working at an ice cream place, and he confirmed what I knew: I had worked at Standard & Poor's together with him, drawing stock charts, the summer we lived in Manhattan, and "absolutely not," said Steve, at Baskin Robbins. However, my father again refused to acknowledge my reality, only chiding me for hurting him by bringing up the past.

So my attempts to become closer to my father before he died were unsuccessful. I gave up, and although he lived for over two more years after that discussion, neither of us mentioned it again.

I am left with the memory of him as a very stubborn man,

more interested in maintaining his good self-image, even if it was a false one, than in an honest relationship with his daughter, and arrogantly dismissing my experiences and expecting me to go along with his deceptions. I find it sadly ironic that, while saying that he respected the honesty of those Germans, like my caretaker Frau Teuer, who took responsibility for their past actions and admitted that they had been members of the Nazi party, he could not acknowledge his own mistakes, and chose falsehood and denial instead.

After my father retired he continued to play leading roles in several Jewish organizations in Frankfurt, serving on the boards of the Friends and Supporters of the Leo Baeck Institute as well as the Franz Oppenheimer Gesellschaft, which aided Jews who chose to return to Germany. He was also active in an organization that promoted understanding between Christians and Jews. He became well-known and respected in Germany, and both my parents basked in this status. "I was really proud of him," my mother told me after my father was honored by the mayor of Frankfurt. My father told me that he didn't want to move back to the US because here he would be a "nobody," while in Germany he was a "somebody." He remained active in the Jewish community in Frankfurt well into his 90s, and also became known as one of the oldest internet surfers in Germany, having taught himself to use a computer while in his 80s.

The Vultures

"Naomi, I curse you for what you are doing for me. Your evilness will fall back on you one day; this I assure you, and it will come true. You are the most evil daughter of the world. Shame on you!"

That was one of dozens of hateful messages my mother left on my answering machine. Several so-called "friends" had convinced her that I was scheming to bring her to California against her will and put her in a cheap nursing home. As absurd as her hostile accusations were, they were unsettling. Her actions were even more disturbing, for under the influence of unscrupulous people, she was undoing all the precautions my father had put into place for her care after his death.

I was unprepared for this, because in the last decades my relationship with my parents had improved. I think their travels and exposure to different cultures opened their minds somewhat. Also, over the years single motherhood became socially more accepted. Besides their continued visits to Berkeley, my son and I visited them in Frankfurt, and we even took a trip to Switzerland together. Although my father continued to believe that in my younger days I had been irresponsible and selfish, as exemplified by my leaving his Dairy Queen, he seemed to respect my advanced degree and career successes. He often asked my opinion about their or their friends' ailments and medications. We managed to avoid discussing Israeli politics, and it only came up when one of their friends, to whom they had given my Chiron email in case of emergency, persisted in sending me right-wing propaganda there. Since the mid-1990s, my parents had entrusted me with several powers of attorney in order to manage their care when they got older, and after my father died I was sending monthly payments for my mother's bills at the Frankfurt assisted living facility where she resided.

For a while after my father died, I got a chance to become closer to my mother. While her husband was alive, she had been his shadow and always sided with him in any conflicts between him and me. After his death, she was willing to talk about the past more honestly. I asked my mother if she could understand why I left the Dairy Queen. Her answer stunned me: "We should never have made you work there. That was one of the biggest mistakes we made in our lives." I felt the wall that had been between my mother and me come crumbling down, and all the past resentments fade away.

I'm very grateful for that short time of closeness with my mother. Unfortunately it didn't last long, for dementia and self-serving people who took advantage of the situation brought out the worst in her, and she again reverted to her old habit of shifting the blame for any problems onto me.

Soon after my father died, a distant relative-by-marriage living in Austria started visiting my mother every few weeks. At first I thought she was being kind and thanked her. She declined my offers of payment, but then I saw large withdrawals on my mother's account statements at the times of her visits, as well as the taking of valuable family gold heirlooms, even those which had Hanan's, Lina's, and my name engraved on them. She also got my mother to give her power-of-attorney at one of her banks. When I tried to stop this, she resorted to incessantly badmouthing me to my mother. At the time I was taking care of my mother's taxes, for she had received letters from the IRS saying she owed back income taxes and needed to pay them. This woman and another "friend," the same man who had sent me offensive email to Chiron, did everything they could to block me. They convinced my mother that she was "tax exempt," even after I explained that everyone had to pay taxes and that she needed to declare all her foreign accounts as well. A US tax lawyer wrote my mother that if she didn't comply with the IRS demands, she would lose everything she had, including the apartment where she lived, to massive fines for tax evasion. German tax advisers said she also owed the German government a large amount of back taxes. Yet my mother's so-called friends manipulated her to mistrust me and not send me statements I needed to complete this work. When my mother started saying they had advised her to revoke the power of attorney I needed to pay the taxes in her name, I got very worried. I knew she would be in big trouble if she revoked it before I could pay the German and US governments what she owed. I wrote the German court about the situation. The "friends" then convinced my mother that I had written the court just to ruin her reputation.

I tried writing these people many times, explaining why I had to pay the taxes and do the other things I was doing for my mother, and begging them for my mother's sake to stop turning her against me, for this situation was making my mother very upset and unhappy. All of my letters to these people were either contemptuously dismissed or else completely ignored.

I went to visit my mother a number of times after my father died, several times together with my son. Once we had to cancel because she was so incensed against me that she left me massages on my answering machine telling me not to come because she did not want to see me and would give instructions at the home not to let me in.

The Austrian woman even wrote the court a libelous letter about me. I disproved all her lies with documentary evidence that I sent the court. Other people also reported the true situation to the court. A bank manager provided an affidavit that showed that what this woman had written about the situation was false. Other account managers confirmed that I had been sending my mother her monthly payments, which the woman had claimed I had not done. All the lies she had written were confirmed to be false. Many family friends as well as my son and my cousin Ernie wrote the court supporting me and stated that my parents had never mentioned this woman while my father was alive. The court issued a statement confirming that I had acted in my mother's best interests by taking care of her taxes and continuing to send her money for her monthly expenses.

I believe that these persons wanted my mother to think I harmed her because they wanted to get me out of the picture for their own greedy interests. My German lawyer informed me that unlike the US, Germany has no laws against elder emotional or financial abuse. These ruthless people succeeded in getting my mother to revoke the power of attorney she had given me to do her taxes, as well as the powers of attorney my parents had given me when my father was alive. Fortunately, by the time this was done, I had managed to pay all of my parents' tax debts. But now my mother was in an extremely precarious position, for with my powers of attorney revoked, there was no one to look after her finances and send her payments for her room, board, and care. I wrote the court about this and requested that a guardian be assigned to my mother for her protection. To my great relief, the court did this.

Still, an attempt was made to get my mother to change her will. Again, my family, namely cousins Ernie and Jack, who is well known from his long association with *The New York Times*, came to my aid and wrote emphatic letters to these people. Finally, this endeavor to manipulate my mother ceased.

The Austrian has since told my mother that she is too busy to visit. According to my mother's past account records, a lot of money had been withdrawn during this woman's visits. I also noticed during my last trip that all my mother's gold jewelry and diamond rings had vanished. Still, I am greatly relieved that my mother is happier nowadays, and that she no longer expresses hostility towards me. Not wanting her to get stressed out again by another court involvement, I haven't informed the police about the thefts.

Putting the Pieces Together

As I was dealing with the problems which surfaced after my father died, such as the tax debts and my mother's vulnerability to predators, I found myself wondering about my family's history, and started digging. As I learned facts no one had told me previously, I realized just how drastically historical events had shaped my parents' lives and characters, and that this in turn had greatly affected my brother and me. Of course, I had known that my father's father had been killed in WWI, and that both my parents escaped Nazi Germany in time while my mother's parents hadn't, but this turned out to be just the tip of the iceberg.

A few months after my father died, a friend in Germany mailed me a 2004 audio interview of my parents made by the Frankfurt Historical Museum. From this tape, I learned for the first time of my father's strict religious upbringing at an Orthodox school, which had given him a scholarship. "They probably wanted to convert me;" he said in a later filmed documentary, "they succeeded." He told that he felt self-conscious about being a charity case and tried to make up for it by being even more strictly observant than the synagogue required. He insisted that his mother, who was not religious, keep an extremely strict kosher household.

This explained so much about my father, from his disrespect for my boundaries, which made me uncomfortable with him, to his disregard for my health at the Dairy Queen, to his ridiculing my feelings and belittling my mother and me. I realized that his were the patriarchal beliefs of fundamentalist religion. Though he later gave up being religious, some of the rigid ideas stayed with him for life, particularly his views of women. I finally knew the source of his sexism. Being female, I was automatically of lesser value in his eyes. My feelings, welfare, and education were unimportant. All he wanted was a nice, obedient daughter. Unfortunately for him, what he got was first a preteen girl who hid a transistor radio under her pillow and bonded with rock and roll's rebellious spirit, and then a teenager who embraced the cultural shift of the sixties, with its idealism, feminism, sexual freedom, and a lifestyle completely foreign to him. I lived my life according to values he couldn't comprehend.

I also think the stresses of immigrating to the US and working for relatives were difficult for my father, and led to his habit of verbally putting down my mother and me, using us as emotional punching bags for his frustrations. When he finally got his independence by acquiring his own business, the Dairy Queen, he couldn't fathom that I, a female, might have my own valid needs and reasons for not following his plan. My mother twice gave up work that she loved in order to further the path my father chose: First, she gave up her job at a bookstore in Portland because my father wanted to go into the pearl business in Chicago. Then in New York, she quit her bank position, at which she excelled and which gave her prestige and good benefits, in order to help out at the Dairy Queen. My father couldn't understand why I also wasn't willing to put aside my own life for his benefit, and branded me as selfish and disloyal.

Now I understand also the source of my father's deviousness. He lived for many years in Palestine in constant danger of being deported back to Nazi Germany if the British authorities discovered that he had only a three-month tourist visa. Later he had to deceive the Israeli government in order for us to leave, for still being in the army reserves, he had us pretend we were just going for a short holiday. I think lying became a way of life for my father, and he came to believe in his own lies. Maybe my early experience of telling a lie which led to an innocent boy being unjustly punished has sensitized me to falsehood and led me to seek out the truth. This memoir is my way of stating my truth.

235

From my parents' print, audio, and film interviews, I learned that my mother had been driven to marry my father out of loneliness for her parents and lack of opportunities in a primitive land. Then, time and again, she had reluctantly given up her own desires to accommodate him. No wonder my mother resented me! While she gave up her career and self-esteem to help my father, I had insisted on becoming independent and pursuing an education, which she had wanted but never got. I had escaped from the Dairy Queen, which, though it eventually brought my parents financial success, meant drudge work for my mother and the end of her own dreams. "We slaved at the Dairy Queen while you ran off," she accused me.

I realized that my mother had bought into my father's patriarchal values and subjugated her own vision for his. I remembered how she had been the object of his ridicule for supposedly lacking math skills even while she was working in finance, and that she had eventually come to believe that she was stupid, as his values needed her to be. It was only in later years, after my mother had given up and forgotten her dreams, that my parents appeared happy together.

As for my brother, my parents' focus on him as the sole important offspring put undue pressure on him to succeed. Yet this was not his only burden, for it was not just WWI and the resulting patriarchal indoctrination of my father which affected our family so negatively. The Holocaust, I learned, had deeply damaged our mother. Her parents had met a horrific end, and she also lost most of the large extended family she had grown up with. While a few of her cousins had managed to flee in time, the married cousins with little kids perished, as did their spouses and children, as did all my mother's uncles and aunts.

My mother was quoted in the German court report saying very negative untruths about me—that I am mentally unstable because I have diabetes, that I had always been a poor student, that I only held low-level jobs, and that I wanted to put her into a cheap nursing home in California against her will. I knew the Austrian woman was inflaming and provoking this. Still, it grieved me deeply that my mother, whom I had always instinctively protected, had absolutely no faith in me and readily capitulated to accusations against me coming from her mind and from others. This didn't really surprise me, however. After my father died, I found 1980s correspondence between my parents and other relatives in which I was portrayed as defective, while they made themselves out to be the long-suffering parents of a daughter with "problems." In the 2004 interview my mother described me as always being mentally unstable because of diabetes. I had sensed my parents' condescending view of me even when they hadn't said their negative thoughts to me directly. Now I understood why visits with my parents had been so stressful for me.

I believed there was something behind my mother's aversion towards me, going back further than her dementia and the influence of greedy people. One positive result of my mother's rants was that her animosity became so obvious that I no longer doubted her long-standing resentment of me. I'd always questioned my reality in light of my parents' dismissal of it with their claims that there was something wrong with me, but after a year of my mother's abusive messages, I could no longer see her as the kind parent of a bad daughter. The underlying hostility which I had always sensed from my mother was real, and showed that I really was a scapegoat for her problems. But I needed to understand her anger.

As I went over my parents' many written, audio, and film interviews and read other historical sources, I saw that my mother had changed her story over the years until it contained many contradictions. These were not random, but formed a pattern which pointed clearly to her primary problem.

During our last trip to Germany, my son and I went to the archive in my mother's home town, Remscheid. We received a film, *Vertrieben, vernichtet, vergessen* (Expelled, Annihilated,

Forgotten) by Ercüment Toker, a 1992 documentary about the Jews of Remscheid. In it I found the smoking gun I had been looking for. My mother, who spoke repeatedly in the film, said that she returned to Germany in 1937 to wait for her entry papers to the US, which her pen-pal's family was trying to arrange for her, and that she was hoping to be able to continue her education in the US. I now believe this was the real situation. It is only later, in the 2004 taped interview, that she says that they were trying to sponsor her parents as well as her to come to the US. Finally, in the last film, *Rückkehr in das Land, das wir verlassen mussten* (Return to the Land which We Had to Leave) by Wilhelm Rösing, completed after my father died, she says that she had asked them to sponsor her parents to come to the US, not even mentioning herself at all. This is only one of several inconsistencies in the interviews which show her ever more unreal embellishments to promote the idea that she tried to get her parents out of Germany.

I believe my mother gradually changed her story in order to assuage the increasing pain of her survivor guilt, trying to convince herself and others that she had done more and more to save her parents, more than was possible. Her parents being Polish-born, and the US quota system being strongly biased against those born in Eastern Europe made it futile for a non-relative to try to sponsor them to emigrate to the US.

Of course, my mother is not to blame. Her parents did not want to leave until it was too late. Things were still OK in their relatively tolerant community when she was there. She told that her parents still had many loyal customers, in spite of the boycott, who came via the store's back entrance in the evening to avoid detection. "Why are you leaving us again?" the local policeman had asked her as she was about to return to Palestine in June 1938. "No harm will come to you here." They didn't know how things would change in the coming months.

My mother had wanted a career, but the only jobs she could get in Palestine were as a maid or nanny. There were no options for her there except to marry my father, whom she hadn't liked that much. My brother and I sensed her depression and felt compelled to make her happy, an impossible task. My brother again bore the brunt of this responsibility on his male shoulders.

Knowing this now, the vivid early memories of needing my mother yet not wanting to disturb her make sense. Then, I didn't question this way of being; it was just unthinkable for me to do anything to distress her. My brother, even more than I, was carefully protective of our parents. We didn't want to bother our parents or cause them any anxiety, and were careful not to tell them anything that would make them worry. But we couldn't have said why we did this. It was an unconscious, unspoken rule, gleaned from some hidden sense that our mother was disturbed enough already.

I now know the term "emotionally unavailable," and although this is an accurate definition of how I experienced my mother, I wasn't aware of it because I had never experienced anything else. When I came to Africa and found that the air was alive with insects, I realized for the first time that these were missing from the life I had previously known. I couldn't have described their absence while I was in it. Similarly, I didn't realize that there was something missing at home, although I felt no warmth from my mother, and little emotional connection between her and me. I could not identify the lack. I attributed the differences between my family and others to our being from another country. It was only long after I was out of my parents' sphere that it dawned on me that I had no memories of my mother being affectionate towards me. I then realized that she suffered from an emotional disorder. In light of her experience, I believe this is survivor guilt.

When I was a teenager, my mother became extremely critical of me. I think that she was envious at seeing me starting to have the seemingly normal adolescence of which she had been deprived. When I left the Dairy Queen, she was jealous of my freedom, and I became the scapegoat for her frustrations. I think my mother's feelings of guilt about having escaped the Nazis while her parents didn't is the source of her long-term habit of always shifting blame onto me, as she could not tolerate feeling any more guilt herself. I also think my mother's antipathy towards her mother-in-law and her claims that Lina was mentally unstable are also due to my mother's misplaced pain, anger and resentment that my father's mother lived, while hers did not.

Thus my relationship with my parents consisted of a void into which my mother projected her guilt and resentments, and my father his patriarchal expectations and frustrations. But I wasn't aware of all that; I just knew I had to get away.

My brother, on the other hand, tried to make our parents happy by being everything they wanted in a son—good, dutiful, responsible, successful, and a genius. He put all his energy into being this way, but it came at the cost of not figuring out what he himself wanted. I think that's why he wasn't happy.

I left my family because it was an unhealthy home for me. However, my parents were not the original cause. It was two world wars and Hitler that are to blame for the damage to my family. World War I orphaned my father, leading him to seek guidance in patriarchal values. The Nazis robbed my mother of her family and her dreams, pushing her into a life of dependency on my father, survivor guilt, and resentment of my freedom. My brother wound up trying to make up for all that they had lost, while I had to distance myself from my family and their distorted reality in order to explore and create a healthy and meaningful life for myself.

I see clearly now that my parents' reality was warped with lies in order to present a certain image to themselves and others, and that they came to believe in the delusions they created. One of the fictions they fabricated was that they had a difficult daughter who was mentally unstable because she had diabetes. I can't blame them for their faults, for I believe that if world events hadn't influenced the development of their characters so negatively, they would have been better parents.

I hope that these sad legacies, born of tragic historical events, which have haunted and crippled my family, have come to an end with me and spared my son from having them passed on to him. I endeavored to learn from my parents' mistakes and tried not to repeat them, but I'm afraid I didn't learn all the lessons in time. I unconsciously started following my parents' example of taking too much personal pride in my son's achievements in school, music, and sports, instead of in him as the unique, thoughtful person he was. I wasn't as supportive as I now wish I had been during his own teenage trials, when he refused to follow my expectations and a path that pleased me, and this caused a lot of unnecessary pain and anxiety for him and me, and I greatly regret that. Eventually I realized my mistake and stopped acting like my parents, but I wish I'd had more faith in him all along. Fortunately, my son has emerged from this sad family history amazingly well, and for that I'm truly thankful.

I learned from my parents' mistakes and have prepared legally for my incapacity and death, and have also given my son my signed letter stating what a good person he is, telling him to show it to me in case I ever develop dementia and become paranoid like my mother.

Grandfather to the Rescue

At the same time that my mother was maliciously maligning me, she was also vilifying my father's mother. This was not altogether new, for she had always complained about Lina. My father, very conscious of filial responsibilities, had continued to send money to his mother after we left Israel, and I think my mother resented this. I remember how angry she was about having to pay for a second pair of glasses for Lina after she had ruined the first. Being old and absent-minded, Lina had left them on a hot toaster and the plastic frame had melted. My mother claimed that Lina had been mentally unstable, neurotic, and selfish, and now she was saying that the main reason we had left Israel was to get away from her. According to my mother, Lina had never helped out when she visited and expected my mother to do everything. "She didn't want a daughter-in-law, she wanted a servant; and whenever I bought myself a new dress, I would never hear the end of how I was wasting money on clothes while she suffered from poor health because she couldn't afford better food." Hearing this pained me, for I had been very fond of my grandmother. I decided to do something to honor Lina's memory.

In 2004, on my parents' last visit to Berkeley, my father had brought me his mother's album of beautiful postcards that I had admired as a child. There were 291 cards with postmarks from 1898 to 1907, in their original 100-year-old album. I kept the album in a cupboard, but now I took out the cards and transferred them to an archival-quality album, scanned them, and made an online album. I asked an organization in Hamburg to transcribe the old German script. After this was done, I translated everything into English.

I was very happy to learn from his writing that my grandfather was a very loving, creative, liberal-minded person who greatly appreciated the arts and humanities. After Lina writes him that she went to see and liked the play, *Uriel Acosta*, Hugo writes that this is one of the best works that he knows, that he never gets tired of reading it, and that he is overjoyed that she has the same taste in this as he does. Uriel Acosta, a forerunner of Spinoza, was a 17th century philosopher whose assertions that religion was a human invention and that faith should be based on natural law and reason infuriated the rabbis of Amsterdam, resulting in his excommunication and harassment until he committed suicide. Hugo sends Lina a copy of the play, "so that you can remember often the beautiful moments that you experienced at the theater & immerse yourself in the clever, liberal & great ideas of this work."

As I read Hugo's thoughtful poetry and prose, I was very relieved to have found this liberal-minded ancestor, and glad to see that Lina had been very dearly loved. Hugo's writing is often humorous and full of fun. He wrote many poems, some romantic, some silly or funny, playing with words and sometimes including quirky little drawings. The depression that had swallowed me after the attacks on my character by my mother and the people surrounding her lifted as I recognized another kindred spirit in my family.

Happier and Wiser

Now I've come to the end of these memoirs. I still live in Berkeley, the place I fell in love with over 40 years ago. I'm happy with my life here, and except for visits to my mother, no longer travel. I'm grateful for my time in Europe, India, and especially Africa when I was in my twenties. Those experiences and the people I met profoundly enriched my life. The memories of the hard times I went through, especially the horrific year and a half stuck in Israel, have fortunately faded, and now only serve to make me appreciate even more being in Berkeley, surrounded by open-minded people. Just recently my mother has softened her attitude towards me. Maybe her dementia has made her forget her resentments, maybe the letters that my second cousins wrote to the people who had been pressuring her had an effect, or maybe my mother really wants a better relationship with her daughter. Anyway, I'm very relieved and hope this continues.

Having diabetes has helped me to live a healthier and happier life, for knowing I could be cut down by its complications in the future gave me the courage to experience life to the fullest in the present, to live out my dreams, and to seek out experiences such as hitchhiking across Africa. I've had several minor surgeries due to repetitive strain injuries to which diabetics are prone, but fortunately I've avoided major problems so far. I've managed to keep healthy by eating carefully, staying very active physically, and doing things I enjoy.

I still do yoga, swim, and dance. Bicycling is my main means of transportation. I was fortunate to have a job for many years as a molecular biologist doing scientific research, a career which suited my love of solving mysteries and doing precise work. Aside from dealing with my mother's problems, these last years I've been researching family history and writing and polishing these memoirs, started years ago. I like how the patterns of life keep revealing themselves as I put them on paper. I recently started drawing again and doing improv and playback theater. There are so many interesting things to learn and do in this fascinating world; I don't think I'll ever run out.

My parents were very proud of being married for 68 years. In my younger days, I had hoped to find a soul-mate, but the feelings I had for the men to whom I was attracted never lasted. Maybe this was because I was drawn to emotionally unavailable men who, like my parents, couldn't appreciate me. Or maybe I just didn't want to wind up like my mother. I'm glad I grew up in a time when it became easier for a woman to choose independence, for I treasure my freedom.

I like being single, love solitude and am comfortable with my own company. I feel extraordinarily lucky to have a wonderful son in my life, who also follows his own path. I've kept in touch with Steve, who got married and became a lawyer, but still plays the most wonderful music. I'm glad that we've remained friends. I regret losing touch with Silvia, Sidonie and Wilma from Amsterdam, but fortunately I made new friends in Berkeley.

I'm so thankful that I live in Berkeley in a quiet apartment with a pretty view and pleasant neighbors; that I'm healthy and feel good and have time to pursue the many interests and activities I enjoy; that I have a considerate son and good friends. I'm content now with my life, and wish everyone could have it this good and be as happy as I am.

Photos

Facing page:

        top left - with my parents in Israel, 1948
        bottom - with Uma & Hanan, Israel, 1953
        top right - in Wiesbaden, Germany, 1956

This page:

        top left - my passport photo, Berkeley, 1970
        bottom - with Steve on boat to Angola, 1971
        top right - with my son, 1981

African Countries I Visited, 1971–1972

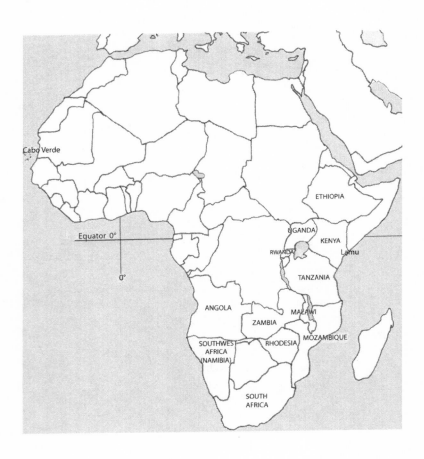

Timeline

1913: My father is born in Hamburg, Germany.

1914: My father's father dies as a prisoner of war in WWI.

1917: My mother is born in Remscheid, Germany.

1933: My father emigrates to Palestine with his mother.

1935: My mother goes to Palestine with the Youth Aliyah.

1937: My mother returns to Germany.

1938: My mother goes back to Palestine and marries my father in 1940.

1943: My brother is born in Palestine.

1947: I am born in Palestine.

February 1956: My family moves to Wiesbaden, Germany.

March 1957: My family moves to Portland, Oregon.

Summers of 1960 and 1961: My family stays in Los Angeles.

Fall 1961: My family moves to Chicago.

Summer 1963: My family moves to Forest Hills, NY.

Spring 1965: My father opens a Dairy Queen.

Fall 1965: I start college at SUNY Stony Brook.

Summer 1967: I stay with Gary in Boston and waitress at a cafe.

Summer 1968: I live with Steve in Manhattan; we work at S&P.

Summer 1969: I graduate from Stony Brook and move to Berkeley.

Summer 1970: I finish my fruit-fly job at UC Berkeley and go to Europe.

Fall 1970: I visit my grandmother in Israel.

Winter 1971: Steve and I sail to Angola, then hitchhike to East Africa.

June 1971: My brother visits me in Lamu, Kenya, and has an accident.

1971–1972 school year: I teach high school in Uganda.

Summer 1972: I live in Bavaria with Steve.

1972–1976: I work at de Kosmos & Arbolito & study dance in Amsterdam.

1976–1977: Back in Berkeley, I learn bellydance, get assaulted.

1977–1979: I work on a kibbutz, then get stuck in Israel.

Summer 1979: I take an advanced yoga course with Iyengar in India.

Fall 1979: Back in Berkeley, I work with mosquitoes at UC.

1981: I study computer programming; my son is born!!!

1985-1988: I study at UC Extension and UC Berkeley.

1988-1991: I get my MA in cell & molecular biology from SF State U.

1992: I work at Children's Hospital Oakland Research Institute.

1994: I work at DNA Plant Technology Corporation.

1994-2000: I teach yoga at the Downtown Berkeley YMCA.

1995: I file a lawsuit against UC Regents, eventually winning the case.

1996–2008: I work in vaccines research at Chiron/Novartis.

2008: My father dies from cancer in Germany.

Made in the USA
Middletown, DE
23 April 2021

37796334R00156